SPLAM!

Successful Property Letting
And Management!

By

David Carter

SPLAM!

Successful Property Letting And Management
ISBN: 9780955977404
© Copyright David Carter 2005/2008 © TrackerDog Media

Published by TrackerDog Media, 118 Ringwood Road, Walkford, Christchurch, Dorset, England BH23 5RF
Email: supalife@aol.com
Enquiries welcomed from overseas and secondary publishers

Please visit the website www.splam.co.uk and www.davidcarter.eu for more information on SPLAM! and other books, articles and projects

This book
is dedicated to
Hazel Elsie Louisa Adshead

who from 1961 to 1996
wrote me the most
inspirational letters.

I miss them still
and always will

Foreword

Welcome to SPLAM – Successful Property Letting And Management, and we hope you both enjoy the read and cull loads of useful information with regard to the interesting world of property letting and management. Please bear in mind that all facts and figures quoted can and do go out of date; housing benefit figures for example are one such case. In other words, don't take any figures as gospel; they are used for illustration purposes only. You will need to check out how they stand in your area, in your time.

Neither can we be responsible for any property contracts, agreements or deals you may enter into. Only you can be responsible for that. As we say several times throughout the book, do your own thorough research and where in doubt, take professional advice. We have taken great care in producing this guide but if you detect any inaccuracies within the work we would be only too pleased to hear from you pointing out our errors.

Why should you consider starting your own property business from home? Because it is quite possible to quickly build up a profitable substantial enterprise with minimal capital input, very low risk, and best of all, you could avoid the huge start-up fees that franchises and linked agencies always require. Many people are earning between 50,000 and 100,000 per annum and more in this business, and you could too.

Won't the credit crunch put an end to all that? No, it won't. Hard times in the property markets are always **good** for the rental sector because there are more potential tenants about, and more unsold properties available for rent. This is the second edition of SPLAM! We have sold hundreds of copies of the first one and there are lots of new things in this refreshed updated version. Thanks for buying and we hope you enjoy the read.

One:

Where did the Lettings Market Come From?

The boom in British property letting began in 1988 when assured shorthold tenancies were first introduced. This enabled landlords to let residential property for a short fixed term in the confidence they could re-take possession of their property at the end of the tenancy. The spectre of sitting tenants had finally been banished.

The introduction of buy-to-let mortgages shortly afterwards by six enterprising finance houses opened the floodgates, and for the first time ever, anyone, subject to credit checks and the ability to put up a deposit, could purchase any number of properties purely for rental or investment purposes.

Since then the graph of property available for letting has seen a steady rise. Even taking into account recent interest rate rises and the credit crunch that has so badly hit property markets in the United States, UK mortgage rates are still relatively low. Yes, it may be harder to find buy-to-let mortgages now than a year or two ago, and yes, investors may have to come up with a larger deposit today but that is no bad thing. You only have to compare current rates with the John Major era to see how far away from those desperate days we are. The proposition of buying and renting out property remains attractive to investors, especially when compared to the paltry interest returns on cash savings offered by the banks and the continuing poor returns available on the stock markets. For many, the buy-to-let market has become known as "the pension". The property market has been, and will probably remain, the first port of call for the careful investor.

It is true that many amateur investors have been baling out of the buy-to-let in recent times, but many of these bought stock on huge mortgages and were only ever interested in making a quick buck. It is also true that many of the seasoned professional property landlords are still looking to increase their portfolios and indeed the current credit crunch will undoubtedly provide them with some interesting pickings.

Between 1991 and 2002 I was the manager of a property management and lettings business and in that time we successfully let and sold thousands of properties across eight counties, ranging from the humblest bedsit, right up to large country houses and mansions. Famous footballers and film stars were among my clients, just as the ordinary Joe in the street. It seems that practically everyone needs to rent a property at some point in their lives.

It makes little difference whether you are thinking of renting out a property that you or your family own, or alternatively, are starting from scratch and aim to build your property lettings business by representing other landlords. This guide has been designed to help you through the minefield that property letting and management can be. Later on we will take a brief look at development and sales too. I only wish this had been available when I started, because I know it would have saved me hundreds of pounds and countless hours of unnecessary trial and error, and sleepless nights. Whatever base you are starting from I wish you well, and every success in the world.

The world of property can be an exciting and rewarding place. Don't let it become a headache or a millstone; there is no need for it to be so. Have fun with it; build it up at your own pace, and who knows where it might lead?

You only have the one working life, on this planet at least, so set your goals high and never lose sight of them. Promise yourself you will enjoy every minute of it, even the difficult days, (and yes there will be plenty of those too!). Retain your sense of humour at all times for if you can do that, you will have great fun, meet many new and interesting people, and you'll probably end up with many more friends than you began with, not to mention a great deal more money in your bank account.

TWO:
Getting Started

The first thing you need to decide before you start your business is your trading style. I'm assuming that you're not launching a PLC. That leaves you with three clear options.

- Sole Trader, e.g. John Smith trading as Oak Properties
- Limited Company, e.g. Oak Properties Limited
- Partnership, e.g. Higgins and Harris

As in many things where a choice is available, all three have their pros and cons. If you are starting completely on your own, the sole trader option is the more likely choice for you.

SOLE TRADER

The obvious advantage is that you are solely in charge of your own business and your own destiny. If you want to set out on a particular course or change direction, you can do so immediately without consulting a living soul. There is something to be said for the ability to be able to react instantly to changes in the marketplace. The main drawback of being a sole trader, besides the fact that you do not have a second set of eyes to scan your progress, is that you do not have any limited liability. Therefore if anything should go drastically wrong with your business, all your personal assets would be at risk. This is something to be thought very carefully about before you embark on your business.

You can take confidence from the fact that property management and letting is one of the least risky businesses you can become involved in. For a start, you should never incur any bad debts, something that is a major headache for most other businesses. Property lettings business do not give credit, therefore bad debts should always be kept to a minimum.

But sometimes things can go wrong with any business, the best laid plans and all that, perhaps through unforeseen changes in the market, and therefore it is important you understand that as a sole trader, everything you own is on the line, up to and including your own family home. There is nothing that focuses the businessperson's mind more than the possibility, no matter how remote, of losing the happy home.

LIMITED LIABILITY

The second option is to start a limited liability company. These days they can be set up for as little as 50.00. Buy a copy of Exchange and Mart and have a good look at the pages covering Company Registration. Ring one or two of the registration agencies, check out their websites, most of them will send you a free information pack and you will learn a great deal there if you are not already aware of what limited liability exactly means.

Briefly, the advantages of trading as a limited liability company are:

- A more professional appearance
- Some protection if the business goes bust
- You may pay less tax on your earnings, as you would be classed as an employee of that company
- You involve someone else in your business

The disadvantages could be:

- You cannot own all of the shares, so you have to share the benefits and profits with at least one other person
- You may dissolve your controlling interest, no matter how slightly
- Some additional paperwork is required, such as annual returns for Companies House

PARTNERSHIP

The third choice is a partnership, which in the past was always the traditional way that Estate and Property Agents operated. Do you remember those old fashioned estate agents trading under names such as Jones & Davies? That style of business has become much rarer these days and personally, I wouldn't go into partnership with anyone, other than perhaps my wife.

Why? Well, if I had a ten pound note for every partnership I've seen over the past thirty years who have eventually fallen out, sometimes over the most trivial things, I would be a very wealthy man indeed. No matter how good a friend you may be with someone, no matter how much your thoughts and aims seem to coincide with another's, it seems that sooner or later, partners do have a disagreement that often results in a messy and mucky divorce.

Just imagine spending five years with your business partner building up a successful enterprise, reaching the stage where you are managing three hundred or so properties, only to fall out over where the business was heading after that. How do you share out the clients and the properties? How do you divide the office equipment? Who keeps the office or shop premises? And indeed who keeps the trading name and the website and bank accounts? Disputes of that nature inevitably end up in the hands of the lawyers. And who is the winner? They are! Every time.

Partnerships also have unusual and peculiar tax rules and you would need to discuss that with your accountant before you set out on that route. So there is your first business decision. Is it to be: Sole trader, limited company, or partnership? The choice, as they say, is yours.

PREMISES

Your next decision revolves around the premises you intend to use. Again there are three obvious choices, always assuming that you don't have suitable premises already. They are:

1. Trade from home

2. Rent an office
3. Rent a shop

TRADING FROM HOME

It is a realistic possibility to start trading from home, and the advantages are obvious, particularly:

1. Low overheads with no rental costs
2. No travelling to and from work
3. Other members of the family could answer the phone while you are out

And the downside?

1. Some clients may perceive it as a lack of professionalism
2. The phone might ring late at night
3. Visitors may seek you out, and at the most unlikely and inconvenient times

The advantages speak for themselves and many growing property groups such as Martin & Co, Belvoir, and Link-Up offer start from home packages, and they do that because it works.

As for the disadvantages, the phone will sometimes ring when you don't want to take calls, perhaps during your favourite TV programme, perhaps during dinner and although you may say, "I won't answer it", I'll bet you do. As for callers wandering up the garden path, they will seek you out wherever you may be, and of course they will often arrive at the most inopportune moments. It's sod's law, isn't it?

Despite that it is a feasible and realistic choice. I know that for an absolute fact, because when I first started I traded quite happily from home for nearly two years before sheer volume of business forced me to seek suitable premises elsewhere.

The moment I finally realised I would have to move out of the house came one teatime. The good lady had prepared a particularly delicious spaghetti Bolognese and I was messily half way through the meal, stained serviette clasped around my neck, when the doorbell rang.

She looked at me as if to say, "It'll be for you, I'm not going".

I jumped up and ran down the hall almost slipping in a pile of newly laid vomit deposited by our sick dog. I answered the door, my serviette still round my neck, as I glanced back nervously over my shoulder at the steaming mess.

A middle-aged lady and gentleman stood before me smiling. "Oak Properties?" she said, "We haven't come at an inconvenient moment have we?"
"No," I stammered, dragging the red stained linen from my neck, "no, please do come on in, and don't stand in **that**, the dog's ill".

They skirted the mess and followed me down the hall. I took them into the living room that we normally set aside for entertaining visitors; unfortunately I was half way through decorating it. The curtains were down, the furniture pushed into the corner of the room and the carpets were rolled back. It smelt musty, and it couldn't have been particularly welcoming.

Despite all that Mr. and Mrs. Ridgely became excellent clients of mine, fact is they still are, even though I've retired now from day to day property management, other than my own. The point is this, callers will, sooner or later arrive at a very difficult moment. There's nothing you can do about that, other than smile and move your enterprise away from the happy home. It goes without saying that you must keep your own property clean and well maintained.

Potential landlords are not going to be impressed if your house needs painting; the lawn needs mowing and there are bikes scattered around the front of the house. Naturally enough their view will be: "If they can't be bothered to keep their own house neat and tidy, why would they keep mine up to scratch?" It's a fair point.

RENTING AN OFFICE

Sooner or later it's likely that you will decide to rent an office away from your home and when you do that, make sure you bear these points in mind:

You Want:

1. Ample free local parking
2. Good security
3. Pleasant area
4. Room to expand
5. Reasonable rental

6. View several possibilities
7. A prestigious postal address
8. Easy to find

These may all seem incredibly obvious but when you are running around desperate and eager to set up a new business or settle into new enlarged premises, it is very easy to overlook the most obvious things.

Be particularly wary of:

1. Long term leases
2. Full repairing and insuring leases
3. Sharing offices with unknown people
4. Service and supplementary charges

Adequate free parking is an essential requirement. You cannot be working satisfactorily if you are forever glancing through the window checking on the whereabouts of traffic wardens. Good security too is a must; if the office is accessed through one flimsy door you can expect to arrive one morning to see it kicked in and your gleaming new computer system containing all your precious files missing.

A pleasant area is not too much to ask. Remember, if it is a rough area and <u>you</u> don't feel comfortable there, not only is your office security at risk, but if you are uncomfortable arriving at work, how do you think your potential clients will feel? And how will you feel on a dark unlit January night as you return to the car with a bag full of rental money, in cash? If you harbour any doubts about a location, find somewhere else.

Renting the right square footage is also very important. It shouldn't be too large, because you would be paying rent and rates on empty rooms, but almost more importantly, it must not be too small. If you sign a long lease on a single room, and your business expands quicker than you expected, you are faced with another upheaval resulting in wasted time and expense. Don't forget, you'll still have to pay the rent on that single room too, whether you are using it or not, and long after you have left, if it cannot be re-let.

Some office accommodation is reasonably priced, while others are plain ridiculous. You will quickly gain expertise on commercial property in your area once you have viewed several different sites. The more you can look at, the better. Settle on a good postal address too if you can. I eventually found two almost identical offices at similar prices. One was located at 400 Imperial Buildings; the other was at Back Lane, 2a Station Approach. Some difference! Same overhead.

Lastly, it should be reasonably easy to find. Remember that no matter how much you ask them otherwise, some tenants will still come to your office to pay their rent money, and if they can't find the place, that 1,000 notes burning a hole in their pocket could find its way into the local supermarket's till. Some tenants never need much of an excuse to turn tail and hurry home. Don't give them an easy reason to do so.

Always always be wary of signing a long-term lease. It may look a good deal to lock in the rental figure for seven years, but can you really say with any degree of certainty how you will be doing in twelve months time, never mind seven years?

When you are presented with the lease document, always read it thoroughly. If you're not confident to check it over yourself, pay a lawyer a hundred notes or so, to do it for you. This will give you peace of mind and is always money well spent.

When I was first looking for business accommodation I found an ideal office on the third and top floor of a red brick office block. The lease was a full repairing and insuring lease and that included the roof for the entire building.

The roof needed a repair, what a surprise, you didn't need to be an expert to see that, but worse was to follow; the roof needed replacing. The rental for the office was a bargain 3,500.00 for the year. I might have signed up for it too, until a builder friend of mine pointed out that the roof repair would cost nearly 30,000.00 and the freeholder could have issued the necessary notices to have the repair work done at any time! At my expense, mark you. It just goes to show what pitfalls there are out there for inexperienced people. I passed on that one, and thank heaven I did.

Personally, I would never share an office with someone I didn't know. I'd be too concerned they might have access to my rooms out of hours. Would you be happy with a complete stranger peeking into your desk, into your filing cabinets, and even switching on and fiddling with your computers? It doesn't bear thinking about.

Check out too if there are any service or supplementary charges. Do all of your sums very carefully. Find out exactly what the utility bills are, the water, electricity, gas, and insurance too, and work out precisely how much per month the office is going to cost you. Then ask yourself this: can you really afford it? Be honest with yourself. If the figures stack up, great, what are you waiting for? If they don't, now is the time to consider walking away. It's too late once your scratchy signature is scrawled on that legal document.

BUSINESS CENTRES

Over the last few years Business Centres have become widespread and they do have their place. They always offer what they call "Easy in – Easy out" terms which is fine from the point of view that you can give a month's notice and quit, but always bear in mind, they can do the same to you, as happened to a friend of mine, two weeks after he'd spent nearly 500.00 on a huge new stationery package. Business Centre offices are often very small and relatively expensive, but they do usually offer a wide range of additional services, such as telephone answering, which could be ideal if you are trading alone and are often away from the office. They usually also offer additional temporary space such as boardrooms for hire, for when you have a client you really want to impress.

In the long term business centres are an expensive option. Personally, I would not go into a business centre, but don't let me put you off at least exploring the option. It is important that you are comfortable with your final choice. It is **your** business, you call the shots;

never let anyone divert you from what you think to be right. If there is a business centre in your area, go and have a good look at it and see what they have to offer, then go home and do your sums carefully.

WHY NOT TAKE A SHOP?

Shops are a whole new ball game and you need to think very carefully before taking on the responsibility of a shop. Think about these for starters:

1. Security is a constant headache
2. Additional staff, you cannot leave a shop unattended
3. High insurance premiums, and I mean high!
4. High rentals are the norm in good areas
5. Thieving, it happens and when it does, it dominates your thinking

I had a shop in Chester for six years and I don't think I enjoyed a decent night's sleep in all that time. In one spell the shop was broken into three nights out of four and the shop was in a decent area just across from the cathedral. We installed sophisticated alarms, internal shutters, and expensive locks, but it still didn't save us. Think how you would feel about that.

The phone ringing at 2 or 3 or 4am on a cold winter's morning is not an experience I would wish on anyone. The voice of that bored policewoman is still fresh in my mind.

"Are you the registered key holder, blah,blah,blah, could you come down <u>NOW</u> please? Right NOW!" Lovely, not!

I wouldn't consider a shop at the outset unless I had a good supply of property and a reliable solid team of people. Yes, I know the properties to let would be beautifully displayed in the window and would attract passers-by and might reduce the need for so much newspaper advertising, but oh, the headaches! Shops are for people with iron nerves.

Strangers have a habit of wondering into shops too, often after a long session in the local pub, harassing the female staff, seeking mischief and picking up almost anything that isn't nailed down. One such visitor picked up our new word processing system and when asked what he was doing with it, he looked at it and said "What this?" and with that, he lobbed it across the counter where it crashed onto the floor, broke into a million pieces and died.

He laughed, hurried out and ran away. I chased him, for a bit, until I realised I had left the shop, and three thousand quid of rent money pretty much unattended in the desk drawer. A shop? Not for me thanks, perhaps you are made of sterner stuff! You will need to be.

Three:
Getting Equipped

These days the vast majority of people already have their own sophisticated computer equipment in the house. Whether the rest of the family are going to be too pleased to see it disappearing out of the front door to your new premises is another matter. Either way you will need most, if not all of the following.

1   A decent computer. They are not expensive any more. Just last week we bought a fantastic new Toshiba laptop from PC World for £399! When I think back to the amount I spent on machines in the eighties that boasted about a hundredth of the power and cost five times as much, I shudder. I once bought an office system that cost me eighty grand, yes eighty grand! What mugs we were! It looked like an angry owl with whirling tapes, and weighed like a power station and needed to be lifted into the office by crane! Today, a second and third machine is a good idea too, for backup purposes and to do all those additional tasks while the first one is busy. A laptop can be taken on visits too and that could be useful, and might impress your clients. You could even do a little work in the car while you were waiting for your next appointment!

2   A good printer too of course. Lasers are more likely to be black and white; ink jets can give you excellent full colour, useful if you are printing out property details, though they can be expensive to run. The manufacturers sell them cheap as loss leaders and then sting the users with high ink costs.

3   A telephone answering system is a must, they are not expensive either, and one new client gained because of it, will pay for the machine a hundred times over. You should also consider activating call transfer to your mobile when you are out, but always switch it off when you are with clients.

4   A photocopier is an absolute must. There are inexpensive multi-functional machines available everywhere. Photocopier, printer, and scanner all in one, but they are a little like inkjet printers in that the initial cost is small, but the running costs of cartridges can be expensive. Check out the ongoing running costs before you buy. Consider buying one of those cartridge refill kits too from your local PC store. That could save you a small fortune.

5   Business stationery. With the improving quality of in house printers you can consider producing a lot of your own printed stationery, but it's still very worthwhile buying good quality two colour letterheads, if only for those all important letters to your clients. Remember, you are setting out to portray an ultra professional image, and it will pay you big dividends in the long run.

6   Computer software, accounting. Sage or Quickbooks seem favourite.

7   Computer software, property management, this is optional and something we'll examine in much more detail later.

8   A decent and reliable car is essential. It doesn't have to be a swish new Mercedes or Jag, in fact there is an argument that says if you arrive at a landlord's house in a fifty grand car the landlord might decide, perhaps even with some justification, that you are charging them too much. Whatever vehicle you use, make sure it is regularly serviced, and CLEAN! One agent I knew insisted in arriving at his landlords' houses in a battered old rusty transit van. I have no positive proof it damaged his business, but I'm sure it did.

9   A digital camera. An absolute must, especially if you want to upload photographs onto the net, a method that is now the norm. And they need not be expensive. You do not have to buy a top of the range model. Many people have their own digital cameras already. If so, use it.

12   Your mobile phone of course. I confess, I hate the ruddy things. I hate travelling by train and listening to interminable conversations that always start in the same inane way, "I'm on the train!" As if they are on the backside of Mars! I hate the way people block up the aisles in supermarkets phoning back with the latest baked bean prices.

"The Heinz are up to 49p but the own brand are down to only 15p!" they always crow back, as if they are cornering the Chicago Futures Exchange, buying up the crop. The poor things don't seem to understand that their call has cost them far more than the damn beans! But I do realise of course that in today's market you cannot be without a mobile phone. It will save you any number of wasted journeys; it will pay for itself many times over. And if the road traffic is anything like it is here, you will often use it to tell people "I am stuck in traffic!"

13   A large and good diary, a page a day at least, don't skimp, it will become your bible.

14   Last but certainly not least, a good supportive chair! Don't try to save money by putting up with an uncomfortable chair. It's a false economy not buying new if you end up taking a month off sick through severe backache.

As for stationery suppliers, check out these three companies to compare prices. Viking, Staples and Neat Ideas. You'll find their web addresses in the trade Directory at the end of this book.

That's it for equipment. You now have everything you need and your business name and premises are sorted too. The next step is to set it all up and practice. Photograph your own house and your relation's and friend's houses too, if they'll let you! Try uploading the pictures onto the computer. Were you standing too close or too far away? Were you at the right angle or too far to one side?

And while you are thinking of that, time for your next task: Market Research. Let's get going!

Four:
Market Research

Market Research is an essential requirement for any business. The biggest companies on the planet spend millions of pounds on market research every year and they do it because it pays dividends.

You are fortunate in that your MR will cost you almost nothing in cash terms. All it will cost; is a week or so of your time, a little shoe leather and a few gallons of petrol. And don't forget, once you have carried out your initial research, to make a note in your diary to review it every six months or so. Just because Agent A is charging X on the first of January this year, doesn't mean to say they still are come September time. This is something you need to check regularly, forever. Keep your eye on the ball. Don't neglect it.

So what precisely are you going to research? And how are you going to go about it? Try these for starters:

1. Who are your competitors?
2. What are they charging their Landlords?
3. What are they charging their Tenants?
4. Where do they advertise?
5. What additional services do they offer?
6. What local properties are available, and at what price?

7. What are their websites like?
8. What sort of reputation do they have?
9. What are their weaknesses?
10. What are their strengths?
11. What hours are they open? And most importantly of all:
12. Where can you better them?

CREATE A RESEARCH CHART

Get yourself a large piece of paper and rule it out so you can make a chart detailing all your competitors, their charges, and services and don't forget to leave a column for yourself. You can fill in your own figures once you've analysed the competition.

Yes, I know it is low tech and old fashioned, but sometimes the older methods really are the best. Perhaps you feel a little uneasy about prying into the affairs of other businesses? Well don't! Why? Two reasons.

Firstly, as you become more successful they will sure as hell start taking an interest in you and your business and your methods and your charges, and sooner or later they will look at ways and means to undercut and undermine the new upstart, <u>you</u>.

That's the way of the business world. It's dog eat dog out there, it's not: after you Claude! It's eat; or be eaten. Are you a business carnivore, or are you the carnivore's lunch? This is the free market. You compete or you go out of business, and anyone who tells you differently is talking baloney. As long as it is legal and ethical, it's OK. Don't overstep the mark; you will know in your own mind what is acceptable and what is not.

The second reason is that every large business monitors its rivals all the time. Tesco's check out Sainsbury's who check out Morrison's who check out Walmart-Asda's prices every day. There's nothing underhand about it, they send mystery shoppers into each other's stores to gawp at every goddamn thing. The prices, the décor, the checkout arrangements, everything. There's nothing secret about it either, they admit it, and they would be neglecting their own customer's and shareholders interests if they did not keep a sharp eye on what their competitors were doing.

What you are doing is precisely the same thing. You need to know what your competitors are charging; you need to know the terms and conditions they are trading under because if you don't, you will lose business and struggle to survive. Nothing is more certain. Not to do so would be foolish in the extreme.

WHERE TO LOOK FOR INFORMATION

There are three main places where you can obtain this vital information.

1. The competitor's shops
2. Their Internet sites
3. By telephone

Go and have a look at all your competitor's shops, if they have them. Yes, you will be pestered and questioned as to what precisely it is you are looking for and you may need to be a little creative. You could say you are thinking of buying a buy-to-let property and ask what they would charge to let and manage it.

There is nothing wrong in that, you ARE thinking of buying a buy-to-let property and renting it out, even if you don't do it now, you ARE thinking about it. Ask for their terms and conditions. The chances are they will give you their full fact pack of information and details on everything they currently have on property letting, from lists of properties available to details of gas and electrical safety requirements. It's all market intelligence, seize it all, every last piece.

Take it home and read the lot of it, every last sheet, even the tiny print, for it is all there for a reason. Remember, you are going to become the best-informed property agent in the county. More than that, you are going to become the best property letting agent in the county, in all things. When you have finished that task, no one will know more about rental property in your area, than you. That's your aim, your goal, and you've just taken the first step to achieving it.

Internet sites provide a wealth of free and easily obtained information without fuss. The amount of intelligence you can glean from sites varies from one to another but keep looking and download terms, conditions and fees and any other facts and statistics that may interest you. By the time you've finished you'll need a new filing cabinet to house it all, if you haven't one already.

Occasionally you will come across an agent, a competitor remember, who doesn't have a shop or an Internet site, or their website might be very basic, and you will need to ring these people to find out what you want to know. It's easy ringing them, tell them the same thing as before, that you are considering a buy-to-let property and could they send you details of their services.

If you are intending ultimately to trade from home it might be a good idea to get them to post the details to a close relative or friend, whatever you feel comfortable with, but remember, you do need to obtain that information one way or another. You certainly do not want to be launching your business without knowing what your main competitors are charging, and what they have to offer. That would be unforgivable.

When you have gathered everything together and all the squares on your chart have been filled in, you will have a list of ALL your potential rivals and their charges. You will now also have an idea in your mind what you can charge your clients.

MAKE A PROPERTY LIST

The next step is to collate a list of all the properties that are available in your area for rent and the rental values placed on them. Far and away the best place to glean that information is in the local press. Make an effort to obtain ALL the local publications that circulate anywhere in the area you intend covering and that includes the freebie papers, the weekly paid papers, and the local evening paper. They usually run a property supplement one night a week, most often on Wednesday or Thursdays. Get them all, even if you don't usually buy newspapers at all.

And while we're talking about areas, if you are happy to drive, don't restrict yourself to too small an area without good reason. It doesn't take long to drive thirty miles, traffic permitting, so why restrict yourself to the local ten miles? Remember, you are looking to sign up business, and as long as it is not too far away, and is profitable, consider it seriously. When I started I covered an area of fifty miles from my base and never regretted it. Obviously it does depend on where you are located. If you are in central London or New York you would not do that, but in ultra rural areas you might consider widening the field even further.

Start to list all the properties available in price order on your PC. It's a good exercise and every time you add in a new property and price it will reinforce those values and areas in your mind. You don't need to know the exact address at this stage. Your list could well look something like this. Keep them in strict price order; it's easier compare values that way.

PROPERTIES TO LET

Barton, studio flat unf 500.00 pcm
Willsdon 1 bed fff unf 595.00 pcm
Hartley 2 bed purpose built 2nd ff unf 650.00 pcm
Barton, 2 bed furn terrce 695.00 pcm
Hartley 2 bed unf semi det hse 725.00
Barton 3 bed pf semi det 795.00 pcm

Keeley 3 bed det unf bung 895.00 pcm
Hartley 4 bed unf det hse 995.00
Bromton 4 bed fully furn det 1050.00 pcm
Narkville 4 bed fully furn det s/pool 1500.00 pcm
Grandiosa 6 bed detached farmhouse 1850.00 pcm

Of course these properties are not yours, not yet they aren't, that's irrelevant, but you are adding to your expertise of the local property market. Get to learn all the shorthand; the abbreviations, they are easy. There is nothing difficult about it. Unf, pf, ff, are obviously unfurnished, part furnished, and fully furnished. Fff is first floor flat, pcm is per calendar month, you'll soon get the hang of the property speak, and just to make sure you do, there's a list of terms and abbreviations at the end of this book.

Incidentally I've studied the pricing of rental property throughout the country and in the vast majority of areas, properties are priced on a calendar monthly basis. There are exceptions to this of course; London being the obvious one, where prices are invariably charged on a weekly basis and are often the same as the prices being charged in the provinces per month! In recent times I have noticed that some provincial agents are switching to quoting weekly rental figures too. Perhaps they think the cash required looks more affordable that way, perhaps they are trying to emulate their metropolis based cousins, whatever the reason, just make sure that you are always comparing like with like.

Charging rental on a four-weekly basis is a different beast altogether and is becoming quite rare these days. It is downright confusing. The public see it as a way that greedy landlords have of squeezing an additional rental payment from the tenant every year, and they have a point. Where rent is charged on a four-weekly basis it is probably to do with housing benefit type properties. Get it clear in your own mind from the outset; is it a weekly, four weekly or a monthly figure?

CONVERTING RENTS

There is an easy way to convert accurately a weekly price into a monthly one. It's a simple calculation. Take the weekly price, say 90.00, multiply it by 52 (to give you a price per YEAR), and then divide the answer by 12 to give you the exact equivalent monthly figure.

Thus 90.00 per week becomes 4,680.00 per year.
Divided by 12 = 390.00 per calendar month.

Note: Never multiply a weekly rental figure by 4 to give a monthly figure. If you do that, you will cost your client, (the landlord or yourself) 4 weeks rental in a year. To make it easier for you there's a table at the end of this book that gives you at-a-glance conversions.

If you are outside of London, try and run your business on a per calendar month basis, especially if that is how all or most of your competitors operate theirs. The more standardisation you can introduce, the easier things will be.

TO RECAP

You have identified your local competitors and have spoken to, or visited each of them. You have examined their websites and you have a good idea what they are charging their landlords and their tenants. You have compiled a rough list of properties available in price order and already you are beginning to get a feel for the local rental market. You now know which areas are designated more expensive and which are less so.

During your market research you may also have picked up an interesting piece of gossip about Williams & Sons who are opening a branch soon in Halton, or Red Horse Rentals who are closing theirs down. (It never ceases to amaze me that some staff members insist on discussing the most confidential things brazenly in shops in front of the public, as if parents in front of very young children. Do they really imagine we are all closing our ears? That we are deaf?)

But most importantly of all, you have identified one or two agents who seem a little complacent, perhaps tired even. May be they are charging a little too much, and are doing too little for it? No doubt it will be from these vulnerable agents where you will eventually take a proportion of your new business. There is no need to target specifically a particular agent. If there is an agency that doesn't quite cut the mustard, you will annexe a slice of their business almost unknowingly.

LIASE WITH THE MEDIA

The next task is to speak to local newspapers and magazines, both paid and free papers that carry property advertising, and ask for their advertising rate cards. Tell them you are just starting in business and ask for a special introductory deal. You can be a little cheeky, mention the Herald has already offered a 33% discount on your first booking, and surely the Post could better or match that.

One thing is clear: DO NOT pay full rate card prices. Remember, everything is negotiable, especially advertising costs. The prices publishers quote are deliberately inflated. The papers expect to accept less, and they will do so. You can also ask them to keep you informed of any last minute offers and cancellations. These can often be picked up for a fraction of the cost of full price ads. I once bought a full-page display ad for just £100 when the normal rate was £960! The publisher was so desperate to fill the page, and I could do that at ten minutes notice. When you see a bargain, snap it up!

If publishers get into the habit of ringing you with attractive last minute offers do your best to take them. If you don't, someone else will, and next time you might not see the offer. On the other hand be alert to the possibility publishers will sometimes ring very excitedly with what they claim is a very special deal, but look at it carefully. Is it really that hot?

RULE Number 1: ALWAYS BID LESS

They will often call you after they've had a frantic sales meeting; perhaps they have failed to meet their monthly targets. Sometimes these offers are more bluster than real discount, and remember whatever they offer you, ALWAYS BID LESS! You'll be amazed how many times they'll take you on. Often they'll say something like: "Please don't tell Bloggs & Sons down the road that we did it for that ridiculous price". The truth is they are probably saying precisely the same thing to Bloggs, and anyone else they can rope in.

Bear in mind too, you always have the option to say, I'll think about it, and put the phone down. As the copy deadline nears and the spaces remain unsold you may get a call back accepting your lower bid. Remember, the nearer the deadline, the cheaper unsold advertising space always becomes. Those pages have to be filled with something and they would much rather it was sold at a LOW rate, than NO rate.

Fact is, if you can get a third off the price on every ad, your fourth ad works out FREE. If you can get 50% off through shrewd negotiation that means half of your ads will run for FREE. Newspaper Publishers are very flexible. They hate to ever lose a customer and they hate it even more if they suddenly see your ad in their rival's paper. They study their competitors even more closely than you do. Take advantage of the fact. Make the most of every advantageous offer that comes your way.

Once you have completed your media studies you have one last piece of MR to conduct before you have finished the initial burst. Take a pen and notebook and visit every newsagent and shop window notice board in your area, and indeed any other notice boards you are aware of, in supermarkets, clubs, public notice boards, libraries, and jot down the details of all the properties you can find that are to let.

On most boards you'll find at least one property and sometimes several more. These available properties are usually from private landlords and they do provide interesting and valuable MR. These houses and flats are not YOUR properties, not yet anyhow, but neither are they another agents, and with a little bit of effort they could become YOUR properties. Take the details home and list them in your diary and save them for another day.

Keep an eye out for potential tenants here too. Just this morning I noticed this advert appear in my local Post Office window. "Retired Couple, good references, seek a bungalow for two year rental term. No pets, Non smokers. Tel: 01425 000000."

It is a very cost effective way of locating new clients and customers, landlords and tenants, so always make a note of anything you see like that.

Five:
Your Services, Fees & Literature

Most property letting and management agents offer two basic services. They are:

1. Find a tenant only
2. Find a tenant AND manage the property on an ongoing basis

There are many other potential income streams that can be added such as inventory preparation, repairs, insurance, solving landlords disputes and others too, but the two listed above are the main planks of most letting agents' business and they will provide the bulk of your income too.

You need to set your prices, bearing in mind, but not desperately discounting, your competitors. You do **not** need to discount your competitors' prices and for very good reasons.

<u>YOU ARE VATLESS!</u>

Firstly, as you have just started to trade, your turnover cannot possibly be above the £67,000 minimum turnover figure (at the time of writing) required before registration for VAT becomes compulsory. Whatever your fees are, they are VAT FREE! The chances are your competitors will be charging VAT as an extra at the foot of their bills. This gives you an instant and immediate 17.5% advantage over almost all of your rivals from day one. It's an important advantage too, so USE it to the full and I'll show you how to do precisely that later on. The vast majority of landlords cannot reclaim the VAT because they are not VAT registered either so a VAT free agent as you will be, is a definite attraction to them.

Some agents charge a flat fee to find a tenant only, say £275. Others may charge half of a month's rental, or the equivalent of 3 weeks rent. That's what I charged and I never experienced a problem with landlords accepting that figure. Set your fees as **high as you possibly can**, so long as they remain competitive. Remember, half a month's rental on an £850 pcm property is a heck of a lot better than having a fixed fee of £275.

FIXING YOUR MANAGEMENT COMMISSION

For ongoing management most agents charge a percentage figure ranging from 8% to 15% of the collected rental. I suspect that 10% will be a commonly quoted rate in your area. If that is widely quoted by your competitors I suggest you set your price at that rate too. Again, you are VAT FREE, so you are already operating at a serious discount to most of your rivals. There should be no need to reduce the percentage rate at all.

On managed properties you may also be able to charge a modest fee when the property is let as well as the percentage. I always charged a flat fee of £100 and then 10% on the entire collected rental. I cannot set your fees for you. I have no experience of your area, your markets, or your competitors, but I would strongly urge you not to charge too little. It isn't necessary. Remember, many more businesses close down because they are charging too little, rather than too much. Underselling yourself is the quickest way to the poor house.

And another thing, if you have a particularly attractive client, and I don't mean a pretty face, I'm talking commercially here, someone who may have three or four properties to let, you can always reduce your price a little by offering a quantity discount. That's fair enough. You can always reduce your fees from your starting level, but it is very difficult to increase them if you discover you've set them too low in the first place.

PREPARE YOUR WRITTEN MATERIAL

You've set your fees and the next task is to prepare the written material you'll want to mail to potential landlords after they contact you. These details need to be neat and tidy, and spot on. It is not necessary for you to fork out many hundreds of pounds on glossy brochures and files. It is far more important the details are neat, with clear grammar and NO spelling mistakes and the content is up-to-date and correct.

Learn how to spell 'accommodation' if you don't know already. The easy way to remember that one is, it's double M AND double C. I am constantly amazed how many well-established estate and letting agents cannot spell the word, and not just the small independents either. Don't believe me? Take a trawl through some of the big property websites and you'll soon see what I mean.

When I first set up my landlord's details I made the mistake of trying to be all things to all people and tried to cover every possible property fact and requirement. When I'd finished my brochure resembled a telephone book with countless do's and don'ts. I listed in great detail all the things I would do for the landlords and all the tasks I would carry out.

I remember one colourful landlord when presented with the tome said to me, "What the hell's this? I haven't read a book since I was twelve and I'm not bloody well starting now!" He thrust it back at me and said, "Just get on with it, it's what I pay you for!"

TOO MUCH INFORMATION CAN CAUSE PROBLEMS

My tome wasn't necessary and in the end cost me money when a particularly vicious landlord took my company to court because one minor item on the list of duties we said we'd carry out was dealt with in a questionable manner.

Fortunately the judge saw through the guy and realised he was only out to obtain a sizeable chunk of compensation on the back of a technicality, and threw out the case, but it taught me a valuable lesson.

I abandoned the phonebook style brochure and introduced a slimmed down landlord friendly version. The landlords appreciated its clarity and we never had a problem with it again. We do, rightly or wrongly, live in an increasingly litigious society and you can expect that at some point someone will examine your brochures with the sole aim of making mischief. The more duties and tasks that you say you will carry out, the more chance there is that one day you will miss something and leave yourself open to attack. Brevity is the order of the day.

Take another look at the paperwork submitted by your rivals, especially the big nationals. Some of them, just as on their For Sale property particulars are becoming slimmed down to the bare bones. Their reasoning is **if we don't include room measurements, we can't be prosecuted for getting them wrong**. There is a strong case here for less being more.

You can be assured that the big national concerns have had highly paid lawyers paw over their details time and time again and you can be confident they are legally correct. I am not saying copy their details, indeed you must not copy verbatim their stuff. But you can take inspiration from some of their work and you can incorporate many of their ideas. And when you have finished your own documentation, if you need a little extra reassurance that everything is fine and dandy, legally speaking, bite the bullet and let your solicitor glance over it. Yes it will cost you a few notes, but you will be reassured that everything is correct.

CONSIDER MANAGEMENT SOFTWARE

Alternatively you can sign up to one of the many property software management programs that abound.

These vary in price and quality immensely, but they do provide checked documentation. I will be looking again at the whole business of property orientated computer programs and documentation in a later chapter.

You will also need to prepare a tenant's application form. These are fairly standard from one agency to another and should not present a problem. When you sign up to one of the referencing agencies they will provide you with a tenant's application form template if you want it. The fee the tenant pays you with their application form is usually around the £100 mark.

Some agencies charge per person, while others charge per application. In other words if a single person applied for a house the fee payable would be £100, but if 4 people applied to share a house the fee charged by some agencies would be £400, and that's a big difference to the agent's profit margin. Charge whatever you can reasonably achieve.

Your market research guide will show you where to pitch your fees, but one word of warning; many tenants will expect a refund of their application fee if they are unsuccessful. Most large agencies do not entertain returning such fees, ever. Some of the smaller ones do. Whichever ruling you introduce, make sure that it is clearly noted on the application form that the fee is NOT refundable (if that is the case). Where this can cause strife is when you have a property that is highly sought after and you may receive a large number, say eight different applications for the same property, and correspondingly eight application fees.

In that case I would never retain more than one fee, and if you decide to do so you can expect justifiable hassle from the tenants if they suspect as much, and perhaps even a telephone call from Trading Standards officers. I don't believe there is anything illegal about retaining all eight fees, but you do not want to gain a reputation for sharp practice. You have to be comfortable with your policy on this.

One other word of warning on charging tenants fees. It is illegal for any agency to charge a potential tenant any fee just to register them on your books. If a tenant rings up and asks if you would keep a look out for a one bedroom flat in a certain area you cannot say: "Our fee for that would be £50". That is a definite no-no. Fees can only be charged to tenants to process their application for a specific property.

ALWAYS COLLECT TENANTS' FEES UPFRONT

Never accept an application from a tenant without them paying the fee upfront. If they say they will pay later, they probably won't. They certainly won't if you don't offer them the property. Be aware also that if they have paid by personal cheque the tenant can stop that cheque at any time until the funds have cleared, and they very well might do that if you turn them down. A cash application fee is the best kind. Cash never bounces. (Unless the notes are forged!) I will look again at processing tenants' application fees in a later chapter.

By now you will have set your fees, for landlords and tenants, you will have produced your own tenants' application forms and you have started to put together the Landlords Fact Pack.

Next, we shall move on to the interesting task of seeking out and securing those precious properties, the lifeblood of your business.

Six:
Locating Properties
& Gaining Instructions

There is no doubt that gaining instructions of property to let is the most challenging task facing any new agency. If you have no property to let, you have no business. You must leave no stone unturned to seek out as quickly as possible property to offer to your potential clients. It is your overriding concern; it is the only thing that now matters.

GET PROPERTY!
GET PROPERTY!

Ideally you should be aiming to include some available property to let in your very first newspaper advertising campaign, and that is your target. It won't be easy, but with a little ingenuity you should be able to achieve it.

Some people starting new agencies seem to think that somewhere there is a directory, similar to a yellow pages, that lists "Landlords", and all they have to do is ring up and say, "Please dear landlord may I have some properties now?"

It would be fantastic if such a comprehensive directory existed, but it doesn't. There is only one way to gain instructions, and that is by hard work and effort. Trust me, it will be worth it. It is a little like getting a snowball running. When you first start rolling the ball it's tiny and inconsequential, but as you slowly get it moving it suddenly starts to grow, then almost by surprise it appears quite large and the strange thing is, the bigger it becomes, the larger and quicker it grows.

Occasionally it can be slow to get started. Don't let that worry you or get you down. Don't let others say: "I told you it wouldn't work". What the hell do they know? They probably have never achieved anything in business in their entire lives. There are lots of people who spend their whole lives standing on the sidelines advising others how to do things. Ignore the doomsayers, and mischief-makers. They are everywhere. **You** are an achiever.

Many new businesses take longer to get going than the owner optimistically forecast at the outset. This is normal. This is when you must stay strong. I once started a business that within ten years had built up a £50 million pound annual turnover, yet I didn't do a ha'peth of business in the first three weeks. Not a thing! Zilch. So don't panic if things are a little slow to begin with. Don't give up, just keep on doing the things we are discussing here until you crack it, because you will.

THINK ABOUT IT THIS WAY -

WHO WOULD YOU USE?

If you had a property to let and you glanced in the paper and saw HUGE & IMPRESSIVE HOMES Ltd advertising sixty properties to let, and beneath their ad

TINY HOUSES Ltd were advertising two properties, who would you approach to let yours?

The odds are that HUGE & IMPRESSIVE would pick up an additional ten to fifteen instructions every week, while TINY would be lucky to pick up just two or three. Why? Because generally speaking people are attracted to success. It's exactly the same with estate agencies. Look in any local newspaper anywhere in the country and you will find thrusting and modern agencies, many of them recently established, let's call them MODERN & CUTE, running several pages of properties, probably in full colour.

Over the page you will find OLD & TIRED, Estate Agents, running a small ad with a few homes in black and white in a dated designed advertisement. Again, who would you choose to sell your home? Not many opt for OLD & TIRED, because people like success. They swarm to success like moths to a light because they believe, rightly or wrongly, the larger thrusting more successful agency will produce the required results. They want the success to rub off on them.

AIM TO BECOME HUGE & IMPRESSIVE

Although your initial task may be to gain instructions, your longer-term aim is to become HUGE & IMPRESSIVE yourself, and as quickly as possible. With careful planning, hard work and perseverance you will become HUGE & IMPRESSIVE almost before you realise it. Trust me on this; there is nothing to stop you.

But before then, let's look at where you are going to find those elusive first properties. Here's where they are to be found.

1. Property you already own
2. Property you are going to buy
3. Property that your friends and family own
4. Your own house, yes the house you live in now
5. The cards you noted in the newsagents windows
6. The small ads in the local newspapers
7. By direct advertising
8. By approaching existing landlords you may know

To have purchased this book in the first place you have demonstrated that you have a real interest in property. If that's the case, perhaps you already have a property to let, may be even more than one, available for rental now, in which case you will include it or them in your first advertising. If you don't already own property, the question must be, why not? Why don't you acquire some?

Despite the credit crunch and ever tightening procedures by the lenders, Buy-to-let mortgages are still available to qualified persons. You will need perhaps 15% - 20% deposit, thus on a £150,000 property you would need to put up £20,000 to £30,000. If you can find that, you are already in a position to acquire rental property, houses and flats that can be offered to the general public.

In recent times the deals and offers available have been changing very quickly. I suggest you google "Buy to let mortgages" for the very latest news and offers available.

If you haven't the necessary capital, or a bad credit record hampering you from obtaining a mortgage, your target must be to generate the cash in order that you can acquire your first rental property. Concentrate too on getting your credit record straight. Just because you might have had problems in the past does not mean you can't put it right in the future. Time is a great healer when it comes to repairing credit ratings. I know what I am talking about.

THE IMPORTANCE OF YOUR OWN PORTFOLIO

Of course there is good money to be made in property letting and management, but don't fall into the trap of spending all your time and energy looking after other peoples' portfolios. Always be on the look out for ways and means of how you can start and increase YOUR OWN portfolio.

In ten years time you don't want to be sitting back in your chair congratulating yourself on how well all your clients have done, probably in a large part based on the efficient and professional service and hard work you have provided. You want to be amongst them, and well up the list as to the degree of success achieved. After all, you will be in the best position to do so.

Why? Because you'll have knowledge of the tenants before any of your landlords. You could pick and choose them, and put only A1 tenants into your own homes. In addition you'll also get to learn of properties that come on the market for sale as some landlords bail out and get rid. It is a constant process. Some landlords are buyers, some are sellers. Many of them are wheeler-dealers and sometimes they will cut you a good deal. Often these landlords are seeking a sharp exit and are looking for a quick sale, perhaps even at slightly below current prevailing levels. There is nothing illegal or underhand about that. If a landlord tells you they are thinking of selling a particular property, tell them you are interested, and ask them to name a price. When a bargain comes along, snap it up! If you don't, the competition probably will.

You will be sitting in the best seat of all when it comes to building your own portfolio. Don't let the opportunity pass you by.

The number of property agents who don't own any property constantly amazes me. When I ask them about it they almost always say the same thing, "I was just too busy to build up my own portfolio." That is ridiculous. Don't fall into that particular trap. Never be too busy to look after yourself. No one else will.

RENT OUT FRIENDS' PROPERTIES

Think of all your friends and relatives. Do any of them have a property standing empty? Have any of them recently lost their parents? Perhaps they have a pretty detached bungalow standing unloved and unattended. Perhaps they have a property on the market for sale that is simply not moving. There are plenty of those about. If this applies to any of your friends, ring them up. Tell them you have established a property letting and management business called PROGRESSIVE LETS and you are looking for additional property to let, NOW. I mean right NOW.

Point out to them if they have property standing empty and not moving, that instead of it costing them money, as it would be, suggest they might consider renting it out, for say 850.00 a month, or whatever figure you think applicable, if only for one year. Stress the monetary aspect. "Wouldn't you rather have an extra 850.00 a month in your pocket?" Money talks, believe me. Paint a bright picture. "Think of the holidays you could have!" If nothing else you will have set them thinking. You have planted the seed.

After a year renting it out they could always replace it on the sales market when the selling environment might be more vigorous. If they rented it out for one year they could receive as much as 10,200.00, less your fees. That's not to be sneezed at, and it's sure as heck better than nothing at all plus bills while it stood empty. An empty property is a deteriorating property. An empty property is a headache that won't go away. An empty property is a negative. An empty property costs the owner hard cash.

I never know why people are in such a hurry to sell their parents' homes when they are left to them anyway. You can only sell a house once, you can rent it out forever, and the rental figure should increase every year. I bought a house in Ellesmere in Shropshire in 1997 from a family whose parents had passed away. It needed decorating, but absolutely nothing else. I paid £53,000 for it. They wanted the cash. It's now worth in the region of £200,000 and it's been successfully rented out every month since. It's my pension. (One of them!)

In all that time someone else has been paying off the mortgage for me via the increasing rent and the house has cost me nothing, other than an annual gas safety check, and a new lock on the garage door. If I needed any additional cash I could go to the bank and they'd give me anything I wanted, within reason, on the back of that one deal alone. Think about it. Do you have a friend desperate to sell a property? Perhaps you should have a quiet word with them and point out the alternatives. The merits of hanging on, the merits, of RENTING OUT. Quote that example if it helps.

The benefits of this deal are there for all to see. So why do so many people rush to sell inherited property so quickly? It's because they are dazzled by the thought of banking so much cash. Perhaps they need the money; perhaps they have never had so much ready cash in their hands before in their lives. They might never have again, and are probably in a rush to spend it. A round the world cruise and an expensive new German car are usually high on the agenda.

Within a few years the chances are the money will be gone. Remember, you can only sell a house once, you can rent it out forever, and so can your heirs, and in the longer term, it will still increase in value. If you know anyone in a rush to sell an inherited house, have a quiet word with them. Point out the merits of letting. In the longer term they will thank you. In the shorter term you will have picked up a very valuable instruction.

RENT OUT YOUR OWN HOUSE

Why don't you rent out your own house? Yes, I mean the one you live in now! That's a ludicrous idea! But is it? Remember when you compiled that list of properties available in your area. Where exactly would yours have fitted in, in the price scale of things? Let's imagine you own a semi-detached house worth say 750.00 per month on the rental market, so what price would it take for you to move out and rent it? 850.00 a month, 950.00 a month, 1050.00 even? Everything has its price.

Take the 950.00 a month figure, imagine for a moment renting out your house for that amount. The first thing you would need to do is find somewhere else to live. But you already know you could rent a similar, possibly even a slightly better house for 750.00 per month, you've checked your lists. So why not move? Yes, you would have some moving costs, but you will be making a clear 200.00 a month profit. That's nearly two and half thousand in a year, and more importantly, you would have another house to let.

Perhaps you could even consider renting a slightly cheaper house for a year or two. Is your present home a little big for you? Perhaps the children have grown up and flown the nest. Why do you need a 3 or 4 bedroom property? You probably don't. A nice little bungalow would do fine, wouldn't it?

If you rented a small bungalow for a year or two for 550.00 a month and rented yours out for 950.00 you'd be well on your way to a 10,000.00 surplus over a two year rental period, and well on your way to buying a second property. We all know that time passes by so very quickly. Those two years would pass in a flash. And don't forget, you haven't sold your own house, you still own it and someone else is now paying the mortgage for you, and you can move back in as soon as the existing tenancy agreement ends, if you really want to. Who knows, you might develop a liking for that bungalow, and the surplus cash.

PRICE IT UP ANYWAY! YOUR OWN HOUSE

Even if you have no intention of ever renting out your own house, I suggest you price it up and prepare the details as if you were. If nothing else it will be very good practice and you now have the very first property to place in your ads. Well done, you're very first instruction, you've INSTRUCTED YOURSELF! Not many people can say that, and don't forget to OVER value it. If you are even going to consider moving home, it must be worthwhile to do so.

If you have a mortgage on your own property you will need to seek permission from the mortgage company before you can let it. This is almost always forthcoming, unless you have a poor payment record.

In future get into the habit of thinking of everything from a commercial angle, even if you haven't been used to thinking that way before. Think cash, think profits, think like a business tycoon, think of an angle where you can make the very best from your assets. Remember, it is a much more realistic route to success by taking a reasonable profit from hundreds of deals, than by making one huge killing. It's what you are aiming for. Many deals mean much profit.

And there is another benefit of over valuing. When you advertise your property for 950.00 a month it could attract quite a bit of interest. Some people will rightly deduce it's overpriced, but other landlords might think, "Blimey, if they can get <u>that</u> figure they must be good. Perhaps they could get that kind of figure for me!"

Landlords are in business for one reason and one reason alone, to make money! They are not a charitable organisation or a Housing Association, they are in it for the cash, and they are attracted by success and high rental figures. Always have been, and always will be.

It is one of the oldest tricks in the book to overvalue properties to gain the instruction. Almost every new estate agent in the country does it in their first month. You can do it too, but don't take on too many at high figures because the chances are you will struggle to get them away. But always bear in mind; your first target is to get the instructions on the book, even if they are slightly expensive. It doesn't matter. Take them on. Instructions always attract further instructions. Snowball theory. Trust me.

LANDLORDS WILL INSTRUCT YOU

If you think you'll never persuade landlords to trust you with their babies and instruct you to let their properties, you are wrong. Why? Because some landlords are so hyperactive they cannot abide to see a new letting agency advertising in the local papers without instructing them too. Perhaps they think they are missing something. After all they don't know anything about you. Perhaps they imagine you are the best property agent in the county and they haven't used you at all. Let them think it. It won't be long before you are.

It's just the same when it comes to houses for sale. Take a walk round any town and look in the estate agents' windows. I guarantee that you will find one house that is in just about every window. Some landlords are simply not happy unless they are on every letting agents' lists, so they will instruct you too, really they will. After all it doesn't cost them anything, does it? No let, no fee, isn't that right? They'll ring, you can be sure of it. Sooner or later, they'll ring you. Be ready.

SHOP WINDOW CARD ADS

The next place to find properties is on those cards you noted in the shop windows. Dig them out, and ring them up. Introduce yourself, perhaps something like this:

"Hello this is John Williams, I've recently started a new property lettings agency, KEY LETTINGS and I noticed your property advertised in the newsagent's window".

At this point the person you are speaking to may well interrupt. Why? You'd need to understand why they are trying to let via a shop window ad to answer that question.

They are using the shop window because, firstly, it is cheap advertising, but secondly, because perhaps they have previously had a bad experience using another letting agent and they are trying to do it themselves. May be the agent did a runner with his rent. Oh dear! It happens. They might say rather curtly: "Never use agents!" or words a lot worse than that. They might even slam the phone down, leaving you staring at the dead phone with a ringing in your ear.

They might also be using the shop window because they believe they know all about property letting and in that case, what would they ever need an agent for? There are thousands of amateur landlords out there. Many of them have watched a few TV property programmes and think they know everything. They don't. Some are very clued up and efficient, but many others are exactly that, amateurish.

Did you ever see an edition of the Tenants from Hell programme on TV where a landlord prepared his own tenancy agreement? He'd entered the figure six next to the months/years paragraph but instead of deleting years he'd fatally deleted months. The result was he was left with a tenant who, not only turned out to be a poor payer but a tenant bearing a tenancy agreement locking him in to a fixed term rental for SIX years. Would a professional agency have made such an amateurish mistake? I doubt it. I hope not. I never did. Nor will you. Amateur landlords make errors like that. One more reason why they need a good and efficient property management agent, like...YOU!

If the landlord on the phone says, "We never pay agency fees", you could perhaps get round that objection by up-valuing the property. After all, if the landlord was seeking 500.00 per month, you would only have to up value it to 550.00 for the landlord still to receive the figure they want (after your 10% deduction). Impress on the landlord again, if there is <u>NO Let - there is</u> <u>NO Fee</u>, so what have they got to lose? And don't forget to, to bleat on about <u>NO VAT</u> and of how much attention you would be able lavish on them and their business, since you are a new, and fresh, and very keen!

Some landlords will see the sense of that and will agree to meet you at the property to discuss it further. Some landlords are just plain curious. Some landlords will look at anything if it might produce a rent paying tenant. On the other side of the coin, some landlords won't have anything to do with you even if you could get 1,000.00 per month and provide them with free beer forever. Some landlords are like that. After all they are human beings, (most of them!) and all human beings are different!

Some landlords are rude, stupid, arrogant, and thick! Just as people are in all walks of life. Thankfully they are most definitely in the minority. But hey, put the phone down, it's their loss, after all. You were offering to advertise and promote their property FREE of charge without any costs or effort to them whatsoever, yet they still wouldn't talk to you. It really is their loss! There are plenty of other fish in the sea. Put the phone down and move on to the next card.

Then there are the confused outright amateur landlords who are only too pleased to talk to someone, anyone, about their properties. These kinds of contacts are rare beasts and need to be courted vigorously. Arrange to meet them as quickly as possible. Look very carefully at the value they have placed on their property. If they are complete beginners it is highly likely their figures might be wrong, perhaps way out, either too much or too little.

If you seriously think you could get an extra 50.00, 75.00 or 100.00 per month for their house, tell them as much. It will be brownie points in the bank for you, and remember, you have no idea if this person owns another house, or another ten. If you could seal a good deal for them on this initial property you might have made a contact for life. If you can offer a pleasant and efficient service, that person may well tell their friends in the Conservative Club or the Bridge Club or the Country Club all about you. You never know where it might lead. You don't know who they might know, and you have no idea what additional telephone calls you might receive thereafter.

COLD TELEPHONE CALLING

Cold telephone calling is a difficult thing to do, make no mistake about it. So do it when you are feeling at your brightest. Smile as you are talking. People don't need a videophone to see someone smiling on the other end of the phone. Don't ever be put off by the boorish replies of know-alls. They live in every town. Develop a thick skin. If you find you get six straight brush-offs perhaps you weren't feeling as bright as you thought you were. Take a break and try again tomorrow.

You can do exactly the same thing with the small ads you see in the newspapers. Yes, some of those ads will be from other agencies, but the majority will be from private landlords, just the kind of people you are looking for. The properties are there, before your very eyes, so seize the day!

WHAT WOULD YOU THINK?

Imagine for a moment that the private landlord advertising in the paper was you. Perhaps you had been advertising the property for five or six weeks, it happens believe me, without any decent response, certainly not from suitably qualified tenants. The property is now starting to cost you money, as it will do if it is standing unoccupied. Then a cheerful person calls you up, optimistically suggesting they could perhaps let your property, and wait for it, may be even at a slightly INCREASED rental figure.

What are you going to do? Tell them to take a bunk? I wouldn't, would you? I'd want to meet that person and talk to them about it some more. If you detect even the slightest chink of interest, try to fix an appointment to meet that lady or gent at their property. Don't fix the appointment for next Saturday, or some time next week; fix it for as soon as possible. What about tomorrow? What about today? What about in twenty minutes time? Enthusiasm is everything.

If it means jumping in the car and going out in the rain to be there in half an hour's time, DO IT! Remember, these are your first instructions and you will DO ANYTHING, within reason, to sign them up. Faint heart never won a fair landlord, or words to that effect. (Whether it is your first instruction or your fiftieth, you should be equally enthusiastic, because if you aren't, HUGE & IMPRESSIVE will be! You can be certain of that.

After all your hard work, wooing hard-hearted landlords, let's imagine you now have three or four properties on your books, including your own. You might have more, you might have less, but whatever it is, don't worry about it. You haven't even started yet.

The next task is to design some neat card ads and get them into the shop windows. You can play about with the wording to suit yourself but I suggest something along these lines.

| | | | | | | | | | | | | | | | | | | | | | | | | | | | | | | | | | | | | | | | | | | | | |

NEWLY ESTABLISHED PROPERTY LETTING AGENTS

Seek additional properties for rental in all areas
Good Tenants Waiting. Low Fees & No Vat
No Let – No Fee. Prompt Payment
Enquire about our Special Incentives
Ring anytime for our FREE Fact Pack and FREE rental appraisal without obligation

SOAMES HOMES
Tel: 07000 00000 (24 Hours)

| | | | | | | | | | | | | | | | | | | | | | | | | | | | | | | | | | | | | | | | | | | | | |

Experiment with your own cards, try two or three different designs and monitor the response from each. Concentrate in promoting headlining features such as: No let No fee, Prompt Payment, No Vat, and Special

Incentives. These are eye-catching facts and hopefully landlord catching too. If a landlord reads that card and has a property he or she is struggling to let, they will ring you. They would be stupid not to.

CAN YOU BACK UP THE CLAIMS?

Let's quickly run through the card and see. Good tenants waiting? Where are they? As soon as you place your newspaper ads you will have good tenants on your books, trust me on that. They are waiting for you out there.

Low Fees? Your fees are low. For a start there's no vat, and if you have to cut your fees by a percentage point or two, to be keener than your competitors on these initial instructions then so be it. Remember, you want the property, and you will do anything legal and honest to get it!

No let No fee. That one's self-explanatory but it's worth emphasising again and again with new landlords. You can constantly reassure them that if you fail to let their property you will never charge them a penny. It's as simple as that. All the advertising and promotional costs will be borne by you, so the landlord has nothing to lose and nothing to fear by instructing you. So why wouldn't they do so? There is NO reason.

Prompt payment. I'll deal with payments in more detail in the chapter covering accounting and handling cash, but this is another very important weapon in your armoury. I'll explain: It never ceases to amaze me how long some agencies hold on to the landlords' money.

Why do they do that? It's not theirs. I wouldn't stand for it if I were the landlord.

One agency in my area actually paid its landlords at the end of the month following the month when the rental was collected. In other words if the rents were collected on the 2nd May that agency would pay their landlord on the 30th of June. That's an absurdity! That's eight and a half weeks! That is Ludicrous!

It's obvious why they do it. They are sitting on huge amounts of cash conveniently placed in a deposit account where the landlord has no entitlement to any interest. Thus the agency picks up a more than a useful interest dividend at the end of every quarter. Remember, we are not talking about tenants' initial deposits here, but ongoing rental payments.

Hanging on to the cash for so long creates a great deal of ill will toward the agency. Any agent adopting such a policy couldn't be surprised if their landlords left in droves. (May be to you?) So pay the landlords quickly. Within 14 days at the most, 10 or even 7 days if you can manage it. Imagine for a moment if you were a landlord previously being paid in eight and half weeks and you heard of a new agent in the town who was paying over the rental in 7 days! Imagine that! Would you be tempted to move your business? Like hell you would! It's a great selling point; tell your potential landlords again and again. They will quickly get it, the benefit: PROMPT PAYMENT!

The Free Fact Pack mentioned is the details you have already prepared and the FREE rental appraisal is exactly that. You will visit the landlord at the house and after inspecting the property you will give the landlord a free and fair appraisal of what rental you believe you could achieve, a free valuation if you prefer.

Special Incentives available. That can be anything you feel comfortable with. Perhaps a 25.00 or 50.00 off coupon that you could design on your own PC. Remember, it's only for the initial landlords, as soon as you have properties on the book you can drop the promotion poste haste if you want to. One new agent I knew gave the first two months management free of charge, and another start-up agent gave away what he described as a free crate of wine, red or white.

The crate of wine turned out to be a box of 12 bottles of plonk he bought at the local cash and carry for 40.00. It was a popular promotion; he pushed it along the lines of FREE CRATE OF WINE IF YOU INSTRUCT US BEFORE THE 1st JULY.

I noticed a new agent in my local paper just this week was advertising: "3 Month's Management FREE If We Fail To Let Your House Within 30 Days". That is a fair and attractive incentive that many landlords would be certain to consider. It's an incentive to both sides. The landlord can be assured the agent would pull out all the stops to let the property, if only to secure their own fees. You might consider trying something similar, especially while you build up your initial register of properties.

Use your imagination to come up with something the landlords won't be able to resist. Landlords are human beings (most of them). They like something for FREE. We all do.

Lastly on your ad card list your telephone number and the wonderful words, '24 Hours'. Don't worry unduly about fielding calls late into the night, you would be very unlucky to receive calls way out of office hours, and you can always leave the answering machine to field the call if you prefer. But you may well receive a call or two at 7pm or 8pm, or perhaps 8am and there's nothing wrong in that.

A lot of part-time landlords work for a living too. They often deal with their paperwork before they go to work or in the evenings. Many of them would be only too pleased to have the opportunity to speak to a friendly agent at 8pm to swop news and views on property matters. After all, they haven't a cat in hells chance of speaking to a national company at that time of day, even HUGE & IMPRESSIVE will be in the pub by then, and that is yet another feather in your cap, and weapon in your armoury. You are available, they aren't.

Place the cards in as many windows as you can manage. If you know any shopkeepers, ask them to put up a card FREE as a favour. You don't need to put them up for twenty weeks, four or five should be plenty and sit back and wait for your replies.

WHAT TO EXPECT FROM YOUR ADVERTISING

I'm going to tell you something now that may seem a little negative, but it's a fact of business life and it's as well you know it from day one. You will receive a very small response to your ads. Not just your card ads, but to <u>ALL</u> your advertising. You can absolutely rely on the fact that you will always receive LESS response to your advertising than you optimistically imagined.

But that's not a problem. It would be nice yes to receive dozens of replies to your card ads and hundreds from your newspaper ones, but it simply won't happen. The fact is you will probably receive only two or three replies over the monthly period from your card ads, but that doesn't matter either. It teaches you two very important things. First, that every potential client must be nurtured and fussed over as if they were your **only** client.

And secondly, that each client you sign up could earn you as much as a £1,000 per year, or more, so it doesn't matter if your efforts only produce two or three new faces, they will still cover your minimal outlay hundreds of times over.

When you are successful in signing up clients, LOOK AFTER THEM. Remember, it is always far more cost effective to look after your existing landlords than it is to replace them with new ones.

Seven:
Launching
Your Business

Up till now your efforts have been geared towards preparing your business launch, but now you are ready to make yourself known to the unsuspecting world with your first newspaper advertisements. You only get one chance to launch your business, so do it properly, and do it well.

You already have the newspaper publishers' media packs in your possession and you have a good idea of the rates they are going to charge. All newspaper publishers calculate their small display ads on the basis of SCC. That is Single Column Centimetres. Imagine a single newspaper column, they may vary from paper to paper, but a typical one is 3 centimetres wide. A tiny box one centimetre deep down by one column would equate to the quoted rate, for arguments sake 6.00.

If you decided your initial ads would be 3 columns wide by 5 centimetres deep you are looking at 15 centimetres, times the rate of 6.00. Therefore that ad would cost you 90.00. They are probably plus VAT too, so at the existing VAT rate that ad is going to cost you 105.75.

NEWSPAPER ADVERTISING IS EXPENSIVE

You don't need to be a genius to see that newspaper advertising is not cheap, especially if it doesn't produce the necessary response, so it is imperative that you get the very best from your advertising campaign. You can do this by:

1. Heavy haggling on the rate
2. Intense concentration in dealing carefully with **every** call
3. Rigorously monitor the response
4. Pick up special offers

We have already mentioned in a previous chapter about haggling with publishers. Be sure you do. Investigate the possibility of series discounts too. Many publishers offer 4 insertions for the cost of 3, or 5 for the cost of 6. Just be careful you don't book too big an ad for too long a series in a duff paper that doesn't produce the desired results.

Don't forget to mention too that you are launching a new business, demand a discount, and if you don't get one consider going somewhere else. I would NEVER book an ad in any paper, series or otherwise, unless I obtained a discount or incentive of some kind. Be tough; remember at the end of the day the publisher does want your business. They hate it if you go elsewhere.

You'll also find a huge discrepancy in the SCC rate between different papers. In my area one paper charges 3.00 per SCC, while another 15.00, so why the big difference? In other words, a display ad in one costs five times the same size ad in another.

Of course it is all about print run, circulation. One of those papers has a circulation of 22,000, the other 140,000, so although one paper charges five times as much, it is in fact a reasonable deal as they carry 6.36 times more readers. You would clearly receive a greater response from the larger circulation paper. The question is; would you receive five or six times as much, or more? Run a trial to find out for sure.

Take a good look too at which papers are carrying the bulk of the property advertising. This is no coincidence. The chances are they have been carrying the bulk of property advertising for many years, generations even, and the local population knows that, and always reaches for the tried and trusted Local Post when they are thinking about property and not the Local Mail. If that were the case, I'd go with the established property paper every time, even if it was more expensive.

Yes, there might be an argument that it may be better to be the only letting agent advertising on the Mail, but I'd rather be among the other ten agents in the Post, because that's where most potential tenants and landlords will look.

MONITOR THE RESPONSE

Monitoring the response is most important, especially if you choose to advertise in more than one paper. If you do that, accurate monitoring will give you important clues as to where to concentrate your future firepower.

It will also provide you with a statistic on exactly how much each individual response has cost you.

For example if you spent 100.00 on an ad and you received 20 replies it is obvious that each reply has cost you 5.00 But if you missed dealing with some of those calls because you were out or too busy, say 8 of them, that would mean the cost of the replies you picked up would have risen sharply to 8.33 each, a huge difference, and another reminder of how important it is to take and nurture EVERY SINGLE CALL.

If you decide to advertise in more than one paper, don't forget to ask the callers where they saw your ad, so you can pinpoint which paper is producing the business. By doing that you can direct the bulk of your advertising spend in that direction in future.

So imagine you have researched the advertising market and have decided to place an ad in the Local Post measuring 3 columns by 7 centimetres. 21 centimetres in all, but you have haggled the rate down to 5.50 per SCC so the total cost comes to 135.71 after vat has been added. But you have also managed to obtain a fifth ad free of charge after the first four have been paid for. That additional incentive has brought the cost down to a manageable l08.59 per advert.

CHOOSE YOUR WORDING CAREFULLY

All that remains is to finalise the wording and email it off to the newspaper. I suggest you experiment with the layout, and design three or four different ads before you settle on the final choice(s).

Remember to include all your strong points, the points that put you above and ahead of the majority of your competitors. No Vat, No Sale - No Fee, Prompt Payment, FREE Fact pack, FREE Appraisal, Competitive Fees, and if you are continuing with it, your SPECIAL INTRODUCTORY OFFERS. Never use the word "cheap" when it comes to fees. You are certainly not cheap, competitive, you may be, but never cheap! Your ad may look something like this:

| | | | | | | | | | | | | | | | | | | | | | | | | | | | | | | | | | | | | | | | | | | | | | | | | |

PROPERTY TO LET

HALTON 2 bed unf first floor flat	£595 pcm
ASHBY 3 bed unf semi det house	£695 pcm
HAMLEY 4 bed unfurn det house	£995 pcm

LANDLORDS: We have good tenants waiting for property in all areas.
No let, No fee. No vat. Prompt rental payment. Free rental appraisal
Free Fact Pack available. Ask about our special introductory offer
Please ring for more information.

TENANTS: Seeking a property in this area?
Register your requirements with us today.
No fee payable until you apply for a home.
Call us now - 24 hours

BRENTS RENTS   Tel: 07000 00000

| | | | | | | | | | | | | | | | | | | | | | | | | | | | | | | | | | | | | | | | | | | | | | | | |

ALWAYS LEAD WITH PROPERTIES

As you can see we've led with the properties we have to let. One of these we may have picked up through a friend, one from our telephone calls to the card ads, and the third might be your own hose, (albeit at a huge price!)

Leading with the properties to let is important because that is the main reason most people will read this page. Right from the off it looks like you mean business, right from the off it looks like you are in business, and an established business. It would be a mistake to run an ad containing no property at all. No matter what the wording was it would still look like "We're new, we haven't anything to let yet, please give us something. Please!"

Be creative. Produce property to let. You can do it, and you will do it.

When you've emailed your rough copy to the publisher they will typeset it for you at no additional expense and if you've requested it, they will send back a proof copy of your actual ad. You can quickly check it is OK and ring the publisher and advise them of any errors or changes that are necessary. I'd always demand a pre publication checking copy. Newspapers do make mistakes, and more often than you might think, and sometimes they are not too bothered about compensating you for them afterwards. If they printed an incorrect telephone number imagine how irritated you'd feel about that, especially on your launch week.

Once you begin to run your own ads similar to the one above you will start to pick up new properties. This is an absolute fact. Why? Because:

1. You are **not** charging vat
2. Your rental valuations are good, especially the last one!
3. There are some desperate landlords out there, with empty property
4. Some people will always try a new face
5. Some landlords want to use <u>every</u> agent
6. They want their property in <u>every</u> advert

<u>WHY LANDLORDS WILL INSTRUCT YOU</u>

Fortunately, from the agent's point of view there are some landlords out there who are living on a knife-edge. They have perhaps extended themselves a little more than they should have done. As interest rates rise you can expect to come across an ever-increasing number of stressed landlords. It's bad for them, but it's great for you. Suddenly they may have two or three properties that have become empty at the same time.

Perhaps they can't afford to meet the mortgage payments. In desperation they will try each and EVERY agent in a desperate effort to let their empty houses, which is where you come in. Snap them up. They might also be attracted to your high rental quotes. Those same desperate landlords have probably already placed their houses with every agent in the district, but that doesn't matter. All that matters is that YOU now have them too.

Bear in mind that your early objective is to let the few properties you already have, but secondly, and more importantly, to add perhaps **twice as many** properties to your next advertisement.

Even if you were lucky enough to let the three properties you quoted here, and picked up three new ones, I would recommend advertising all six the following week. It will demonstrate to keen eyed landlords that you are quickly gaining instructions and becoming established. You might consider putting a NOW LET slash notice against one or two. This creates a very positive image. New properties and successful lets too, and that is a recipe for success.

When landlords call, you know how you to react:
Quickly, cheerfully and efficiently
Speak with a smile on your face
Make an early appointment to meet them
Be complimentary

WIDEN YOUR LAUNCH

Beef up your business launch by designing and distributing your own colour A4 posters. A good inkjet printer will produce reasonable quality posters for very little cost.

Call in a few favours from the traders you use and ask them to put one of your posters in their windows for FREE. The newsagent where you buy your daily paper, the barbers where you have your hair cut, the pet shop where you buy your birdseed, all these kind of traders want to keep your business and will surely put up one of your posters for five or six weeks to do so. Use your imagination, keep a few posters in the car as you never know when and where you might stumble across an opportunity to display your services, but don't illegally bill post. That will only cause you grief. Ask your partner to do the same, and any other friends or relatives who own shops too.

This type of additional publicity will cost you next to nothing and it will gradually make you and your activities better known throughout the town. If you put up ten posters and picked up two new clients it would pay for your time one hundred times over and more.

PREPARE A PRESS RELEASE

Speak to your local newspapers too especially the ones where you have placed the bulk of your advertising and try and wangle some editorial from them. Local papers are often stuck for news to fill out their columns and editorial is better coverage than paid for advertising because that is often shoved away on the advertising only pages. Editorial coverage is free!

Prepare a PRESS RELEASE to give your launch more credibility and post a copy to all your local newspapers and magazines. If you don't know the wording, google FREE PRESS RELEASES and dozens of samples will come up that you can use.

It could be something along these lines:

"Former policeman/teacher etc launches new local property company", or

"Local man hopes to offer employment via his new property business," or

"Local woman returns to the town and sets up new property company specialising in helping students find suitable accommodation," or

"New Property Company opens in the city/town."

Play about with it until you will come up with something eye-catching and memorable. Read it to your spouse, read it to your kids. They'll soon tell you if it's too cheesy.

Don't forget to include your telephone numbers and email address in all announcements so that readers can contact you. Put a photograph in too, perhaps in front of a property you have to let, that would be a real coup.

Tell everyone about it. Spread the word. Local newspapers are usually only too pleased to run a little editorial about local people setting up new enterprises, especially if it will ultimately lead to additional local jobs. Quite often they are desperate for snippets of news to fill their columns. Be imaginative. Be creative. You only launch your business once and you won't have the opportunity to distribute this particular press release ever again.

DEALING WITH TENANTS FOR THE FIRST TIME

Prepare yourself properly to deal with prospective tenants for the first time. If you are not used to dealing with clients on the telephone it might be an idea to type out and print some general notes to help you when they ring. Anyone can forget their lines when talking about a new business, especially in the early days, and you will find it very helpful if you have some general notes handy to refer to when tenants call.

Tenants will ring you for one of three reasons:

- To enquire about a specific property listed
- To enquire after other properties you may have
- To register their requirements

These are the questions you would like them to answer:

- Their name, and is the property for a family, a couple, or single person
- Their address: This is most important if you want to post them details at a later date
- Phone Number: Try and get day, evening, and mobile. Email addresses can also be useful
- Employed: You will need to know if they are working and what they do
- Property Type Required: flat/ terrace /semi/ det/bung/other
- Furnished or unfurnished: Very important to save wasting time later
- When do they wish to move in?
- Pets? Most important, as some landlords will not tolerate cats and dogs, never mind snakes and heaven knows what else!
- Length of Tenancy required: They may want 2 years or 2 months, or even 2 weeks, and you need to know which it is
- Rental Figure: What range do they want pay?

- Smokers: More and more landlords require non-smoking tenants

Some tenants are only too happy to chat and will tell you anything you want to know. Others will be reluctant to give you anything more than a name and number. At this stage, respect their views. There is little to be gained by forcing the issue. They will have to provide you with full and comprehensive details before they get anywhere near renting a property.

Never release the full address of any property to anyone over the telephone without taking their full details and telephone numbers. We had a young man who would ring almost every Thursday from a public call box. We grew to know him quite well and he turned out to be a well-known local burglar. He was particularly interested in empty properties. Once he had the address he would call round, break into the property and steal the central heating boiler or anything else that could be detached from the building. He didn't get any addresses from us.

If someone wants an address to view a particular neighbourhood, you can always give out a street name, but not the individual number. We never issued house numbers until we were confident it was a bona fide enquiry, and the prospective tenant really did wish to book an accompanied viewing of the property.

Far and away the best policy to adopt when dealing with potential tenants is to talk to them as if they are long lost friends, courteous and helpful. Try and put across that you are working for their benefit in an effort to get them fixed up. You will make a great deal more headway by trying these friendly tactics than by adopting an inquisitorial attitude, bellowing one question after another in monotone, what I call the name, rank, number, syndrome.

Of course you are NOT working for the benefit of the tenant; you are working on behalf of the landlord, representing their interests, trying to find the best tenant for them at the **highest** possible rental figure. Remember, the landlord pays the bulk of your fees. By representing them successfully you will achieve results for the most important person involved in this whole enterprise. **YOU!** It is worth reminding yourself of that now and again.

From that first advertisement typically you could receive twenty replies from prospective tenants, half of which may well be suitable for a property somewhere in your locale. You could also typically expect to receive calls from around four or five landlords, as the week passes before your next advertisement appears. Don't forget to fuss over every single reply, especially the landlord enquiries, because they are the source of the majority of your future business.

Which brings us neatly on to the next chapter. How to best woo and convert landlords to dealing with you. It's an interesting and challenging task, but armed with my expertise of visiting hundreds of landlords, you will be well equipped to win the day.

On Tenants to Recap:

Prepare yourself to speak to tenants
Design your own form incorporating your questions
Talk to them as if they were a good friend

Eight:
Wooing the
Landlord Animal

Landlords can be likened to the animals of the African plain; they come in all shapes, sizes, colours, ages, and temperament.

In the old days landlords were pigeonholed into a stereotype of a late middle-aged man, probably with a beard and grasping hands. I suspect that was never the case, and it certainly isn't today. Your landlord is more likely to be an attractive professional woman in her twenties, or a whiz kid businessman in his thirties.

Recently I experienced a huge increase in Chinese landlords and very good they are too. I have always found them excellent to do business with, honest and straight, polite and loyal. If you give them a good deal and great service, they will undoubtedly recommend you to their aunts and uncles, and before you know it you will be representing Mr and Mrs Wang, Chang, Wu, Chu, Soo, and Lu too.

I did, and they were among the best landlords I ever dealt with. Some of them couldn't even speak English but once I'd built a successful relationship with them, they never went anywhere else. The great thing about them was they kept acquiring more and more property and would ring me up and triumphantly announce: "We have another one, you wannit?" I wannit!

One of the reasons behind their spending sprees was a huge influx of capital from Hong Kong where property prices are far higher than here. The Chinese, as everyone knows, have always made excellent business people and they all seemed intent on building up property portfolios at a record rate. Long may it continue!

MEETING LANDLORDS

So the point I am trying to make is, there is no such thing as a typical landlord. When you are fortunate enough to be invited to visit a landlord make an appointment as early as you can, and try and ascertain whether the property you are meeting him or her at, is the property they are considering letting, or their own home. That's most important and I'll tell you why in a minute.

Most landlords will meet you at the property that is to be let; but many will invite you into their own homes. Imagine you have an appointment to visit a landlord at their home at 2pm the following day. The first point to remember is to BE EARLY! I don't mean knock on the door early, just get into the area promptly, just in case the traffic is bad. Think about it this way, the landlord may well have invited three different agents to visit them at hourly intervals. Imagine two are late and one is on the nail, who do you think will get the instruction? Precisely!

I liked to knock on the door at exactly the time the appointment was made. There is nothing more satisfying than being invited into the hall as the clock is loudly chiming the time. The landlord will notice your punctuality, you can be sure of that.

Offer your hand, if they wish to shake it, they will. Incidentally my Chinese friends were never that keen to shake hands and after a while I gave up proffering mine. If the landlord does offer their hand, shake it firmly and briefly. Never offer a wet fish of a handshake, it's a real turn off, and never bone-crush that hand as a statement of how strong and tough you are. As in many things, the happy medium is the preferred route.

Don't sit down until you are invited to do so. A small point perhaps, but some people notice manners more than most. Always wipe your feet, especially if it is wet and muddy. You may have sent your fact pack ahead in the post, but always bring another one just in case the landlord wishes to go over a few points, or has lost their copy. Try and relax, try and smile, be friendly, and treat this person as you would a wealthy relative. Answer any questions carefully and confidently and don't forget to emphasis your USP's.

EMPHASISING YOUR USP's

What are USP's? Unique Selling Points. You know what your USP's are, and there is nothing wrong in repeating them again and again. No Vat, No let/No fee, No Advertising Costs, Free Rental Appraisal, Competitive Fees, and perhaps most importantly of all, you can state categorically that you will turn over the rental payment within 10 days (or whatever time you have set). Just make sure you adhere to that. There's nothing worse than an agent promising to pay rental within 10 days, only for the landlord to be still waiting 30 days later. That stinks of trouble.

By the way, just make sure you word that correctly. You are not promising to turn over the rental in 10 days from the date it is due, say the first day of the month, you are promising to turn it over within 10 days of IT BEING COLLECTED. That's an important difference, because the tenant may sometimes pay a little late. Your USP's may not be unique individually, but put together the package you are offering probably will be.

If you are competing against big national agents, you can do so with confidence. They will never be able to compete with you on flexibility of terms. You can change your prices, or anything else, at the drop of a hat. They could need seven committee meetings and refer to Head Office before they could change anything of theirs.

You can also react to changes in market conditions far quicker than they will. Always be on the look out for that. Steal a march on the rivals at every opportunity. Keep abreast of industry developments. You will become known for it. "So and so is always on the ball", that is the reputation you should aim to achieve.

I mentioned before about trying to ascertain whether the property you were visiting was the property to be let. The reason for that is simple. If it were the property to be let, you have an easy and early opportunity to value the rental figure. Firstly, you could drive past and check out the neighbourhood and the exterior condition of the property. Secondly you may notice two or three similar properties in the neighbourhood to let. You could hurry back to the office and check out the rental figures. It's obviously much easier to reach an accurate rental figure if you already know what three or four similar properties in the same road are on the market for.

DISCLOSING YOUR VALUATION

When a landlord asks for your valuation give it to them straight. Don't prevaricate. You can perhaps justify your figure by adding: "Number 19 up the road is on the market for 550.00, but that one is not centrally heated. Yours is a slightly better property, hence the figure of 595.00".

What you are really telling them is that you have done your research, you have your finger on the pulse, and you know what is going on. You haven't simply plucked a figure out of thin air and hoped for the best.

The landlord should be impressed. Hopefully he or she has liked your demeanour, your valuation was spot on, and they were particularly pleased with your trump cards of No Vat and Early Payment. They were so pleased they might even instruct you there and then to get on with it. This is not unusual. I have been instructed hundreds of times on site within ten minutes of meeting a complete stranger.

I have been issued with keys on numerous occasions to properties worth over half a million pounds within ten minutes of meeting a complete stranger for the first time. It's a nice feeling to realise they had enough confidence in you for them to do that. You will feel the same. The more often you are instructed, the more confident you will become in the future.

If they are instructing you to let their property it is important to agree the viewing arrangements. They will be one of these:

1. The landlord will give you a key, be sure to check if there is an alarm system. If there is, make sure you obtain the code

2. The landlord will meet any potential viewers on site. In that case make sure you attend too. If you don't, the landlord might strike a private deal behind your back with the tenant. (They wouldn't do that would they? They might, if you gave them the opportunity.)

3. The landlord will arrange for someone else to open up. Again, you should attend. Why? Because you can hand the potential tenant an application form. You might even be able to collect the application fee there and then. If you do, it will be the first fee you ever collect. Money is the incentive. Go to ALL viewings in person.

NOTES ON BURGLAR ALARMS

Burglar alarms are very commonplace and increase the security of any property, but they can be a real nuisance for agents, especially if you forget about the alarm. There is nothing worse than opening a property with a keen viewer on your shoulder, only to hear that beep-beep-beep as you realise that you have forgotten about the alarm or worse still, that the landlord had not bothered to tell you about it at all. In some areas perhaps half of all houses have alarms, so always go prepared.

Most alarms are one of two types, either code, usually four digits, or key, where you simply insert the key in the alarm and turn it off. Here's a tip if you unexpectedly hear the dreaded beeps and have no code:

Most codes are either a famous date, the landlord's birth year for example, which you are unlikely to know, or the one date that everyone knows, 1066. You will be surprised at how often that is the code. It's worth a try. But there is another code that comes up time and time again. That is 0123. Why? Because that is the default code that the system is supplied with and many owners never bother to reset it. So try 0123 and you might be lucky. If it's a key type, many cheaper systems use a small key like a filing cabinet key. In fact they are so alike that they will often do the job for you. That might be worth a try too, so if you have a similar key on your ring, try it.

If that fails you should be able to sort the problem via your mobile phone and hopefully before the police arrive!

CONFIRMING INSTRUCTIONS

Once instructed, return to your office and write a letter to the landlord, in duplicate, confirming their instruction to you to let the property. Confirm the ASKING rental, and remind the landlord that a Gas Safety Certificate will be necessary. (Lots more on that topic later).

Open an individual file for the property, those large multi coloured cardboard document wallets are excellent for the purpose. You can place copies of all correspondence in the file as you proceed. You can also note any telephone calls you make in there relating to the property, and keep all relevant paperwork together tidily in one place.

Make sure before you take the matter any further you have the landlord sign the second copy of your letter and return it to you as an acknowledgement. This is most important, without it you have nothing in writing that instructs you to proceed. If you sign up for one of the software packages, these letters are all automatically generated for you.

You may be instructed there and then, but the chances are you won't be. Return to the office and hope the phone rings over the next day or three. Even after that, you don't need to write the property off. I have been instructed up to nine months after visiting a landlord. They explained they had been decorating the house and they liked to do it at their own speed until everything was just so.

But if you don't hear anything further, or are convinced you failed to win his or her trust, try and analyse why you didn't get the instruction, where you went wrong, especially if the very next week you notice the property appearing in your rival's advertisement. Spit!

REASONS FOR FAILURE

Why did you fail to land the instruction? Could it be one of these?

1. Your rivals valued it higher (even if it was unrealistic). There's nothing you could have done about that. If it is badly overvalued you can be sure it will be tricky to let. If they struggle to let it, which they will, it may well come back to you.
2. The landlord didn't like you. (Hey it happens. None of us likes everyone, that's human nature). Forget about it. There are far more fish in the sea.
3. You stumbled over answering questions. (Well you won't do that again.)
4. The landlord got cold feet about letting at all. (Yep, that happens too. There is nothing you can do about that either).
5. You were late. (That is unforgivable!)
6. The landlord was a timewaster and really only wanted to pick your brains before trying to let it themselves. (Yes, that happens too sometimes, and you will probably recognise it when it does. All you can do is be helpful and polite and leave as quickly as you can to pursue other business.)

If you can successfully analyse why you didn't get the instruction, you will improve your chances of being successful next time. Remain optimistic. Tell yourself; it is their loss, because it is!

HOW TO IMPRESS YOUR LANDLORDS

You can always impress your landlords by being:

1. On time
2. Cheerful and optimistic. Smile
3. Never proffer a limp handshake, nor a bone-crusher
4. Shine your shoes, and look smart. No trendy unshaven look
5. Avoid garlic breath, and alcohol fumes too
6. Give them your undivided attention. Turn off your mobile phone
7. Be complimentary, but never fawning, about their house, their children, their pets, their choice of décor and art, and anything else that catches your eye
8. Emphasise your USP's and be enthusiastic
9. Stress the positives and ignore the negatives. Never say: "the market is slow". The market is always slow for losers. For winners like you, every day is a busy day
10. Fresh deodorant please. We can all pong dreadfully after a hectic busy day, especially in summer. Keep a supply in the car
11. Do your homework. To do otherwise is unforgivable
12. Don't make promises you can't keep. If you say the property will be let in 48 hours, you will simply look foolish if it is still empty two weeks later
13. Never rubbish the competition. This is a cheap shot, and may simply rub the landlord up the wrong way. They may be related to other agents. They may have many properties successfully let through them. Perhaps they are simply giving you a chance. They could be really miffed with you, even if they don't show it
14. Be businesslike in all things, but not overly familiar
15. And never smoke. Too stupid I know, but I have seen an agent do that

Abide by these pointers and you will greatly increase your chances of being instructed, even if it is several weeks or months down the line.

In the next section we'll look in detail at valuing properties and preparing property information sheets. It's an important task, and it needs to be carried out accurately.

Nine:
Rental Valuations & Property Spec Sheets

There is a great deal of bumf written about valuing property for rental purposes as if there were some accurate equation based on the square footage times the length of the tenancy, or some such crazy mathematical formula.

That may be the case in valuing properties for sale in Knightsbridge, but for rentals, in my opinion, no such formula exists. The value of a property for rental purposes is precisely the same as for anything else. It is worth what you can persuade someone to pay for it. And I don't mean to sign a contract at a certain figure, I mean to actually PAY THE CASH.

<u>ESTABLISHING THE ASKING RENTAL FIGURE</u>

Setting property rental values with confidence comes with experience. The more you do it, the easier it becomes. And don't forget, this applies just as much to valuing your own property, as it does for others.

If you are unsure about a valuation, you can always say to the landlord: "Did you have a figure in mind?" I personally don't care for that strategy as it smacks of lack of confidence, but occasionally it might be the right path if you are especially unsure.

Most landlords <u>will</u> have a figure they want, and many will tell you, but there are always those that say, "You're the expert, you tell me". That's fair enough. They are right. The fact is, if you've done your homework, as you should have done, you will KNOW an accurate figure BEFORE you visit the house. You can always adjust it up or downward once you have inspected the inside of the property, once you have seen the lie of the land.

At least you won't have the problem a friend of mine had; he's an Estate Agent in Canford Cliffs in the leafy suburbs of Bournemouth. He was invited to value a modern home on the trendy Sandbanks peninsula. Fortunately the vendor was a friend of his and when he was asked for his valuation my friend said: "It's a difficult one, I could be way out here."

Before he could say any more his friend started laughing and told him they'd already had three agents around the property. One had valued the house at £1.35 million, the second at £1.6 million and the third at £1.95 million! A difference of £600,000 between the top and bottom valuations! Imagine that? Being an estate agent and being £600,000 out! It doesn't bear thinking about. At least on rentals, even if you are out, you won't be out by much.

You can always adjust your suggested figure, for that is all it is, up or downward depending on market conditions. For example, if there is a lot of empty property on the market and it is not shifting, it would make sense to value it slightly lower. Explain to the landlord why you have done so. On the other hand, if the market was strong and properties were letting quickly, you could afford to be more bullish and value it higher than you normally might. Don't forget, there are other good reasons to value it as highly as you can.

Firstly, if you can obtain a higher rental figure you will cement your relationship with the landlord, and secondly, remember, you are working for a percentage fee. 10% of 900.00 is clearly better than 10% of 800.00. It may only be 10.00 per month more for you, but that's 120.00 a year. If you did that fifty times, as you may well do, it begins to mount up. Always concentrate on increasing your fee income, and you don't need to increase your prices to do so. It will help you to achieve your goals that much faster.

UPDATE YOUR INTELLIGENCE

Continue to monitor ALL properties that go up for rental in your area. If you do, you will always have your finger on the pulse when it comes to valuation time. I confidently predict that within one month you will be happily and accurately valuing properties, providing you have done your homework.

Believe me, anyone can do it. You don't need to be twenty years in the property business, or have long lists of letters after your name to accurately value properties for rental purposes.

MAKE NOTES & LOTS OF THEM

When you visit properties always take your diary or dictating machine or laptop and make copious notes. There is nothing worse than an agent having to ring the landlord back and say: "Remind me again, was it centrally heated?" It makes you look a complete Wally, and worse still, incompetent.

If you make accurate notes you will not need to ring back. Dictating machines can be very helpful in this respect. They certainly look professional as you wander around the property talking to yourself.

These points are all important to note:

- Furnished or Unfurnished? It could affect the value, and the tenant
- Does the furniture abide by legal legislation?
- Is there a gas safety certificate?
- Is it double glazed and centrally heated?
- Is there a shower, second bathroom?
- Is the property carpeted, and are they clean?
- Off road parking? Garage?
- Is there a fitted kitchen?
- Number of bedrooms of course, similarly reception rooms?
- When available? Length of time available? One year? Two years?
- Alarmed? Key or Code?
- Are the gas and electricity meters quarterly or coin? That is important, as it is to ascertain who supplies the services?
- Is there a garden? Who has access, especially important on flats? Is there a gardener? Is there a garage? Is the garage empty? Most are not!
- Are there curtain rails? If not try and persuade the landlord to put some up. Not many tenants want to start messing around with curtain rails

- What is the general state of repair of the property? Don't be afraid to ask the landlord to deal with essential maintenance, especially anything to do with gas and electric. Cracked windows should be dealt with too. Have a look at the outside of the property as well. Are there any overhanging tiles that could fall on visiting tenants, or on you? If so, insist they are repaired
- Is there a banister on the stairs? There should be
- Is there plumbing for a washing machine and dishwasher?
- Do the taps leak? Are the bathrooms modern? If so, make an issue of that in your descriptions
- Will the landlord accept smokers and pets? That's always important, as many people will not
- Will the landlord accept students and tenants on State benefit?

For the most part these are simple common sense factors. You need to find out the things that you would want to know yourself if you were renting the house.

The best way to ensure you don't miss anything is to design your own easy to follow checklist. Include all the above features and any others you deem necessary. That way you will never miss a thing. Without a checklist it is so easy to miss items, and sod's law tells you that a potential tenant will ask you the very question you forgot to note down.

It is <u>not</u> necessary to measure the rooms. I don't know of any letting agent who does that. It would add extra work for no benefit, and it could provide the nitpickers and compensation seekers an easy opening to make a complaint against you.

You know the kind of thing.
"You said the living room was 14'6" when it is only 14'2" and my piano won't go in. We want a deduction in the rent".

Who needs that kind of hassle? And believe me, it does happen.

WRITING A PROPERTY SPEC SHEET

When you return to the office you can write a brief description of the property. My advice would be to keep it short and simple, to the point, and above all, accurate. Avoid flowery language, the word "gorgeous" has no place in any property description, and never say anything that is obviously untrue. Your description could read something like this.

An unfurnished 3 bedroom semi detached house benefiting from gas central heating, part double-glazing, garage and spacious gardens. The accommodation comprises hall, lounge, sitting room, modern fitted kitchen, 3 bedrooms and smart bathroom. Outside there is a detached garage, ample off road parking and lawned enclosed gardens to the rear. The property is available now for 12 months with an extension possible thereafter. No pets or smokers accepted. Please ring our office for more information and to make an early appointment to view.

That's 84 words or thereabouts and in my opinion if you exceed say 150 words, on a letting, you're probably including too much detail. That really is all you need, a basic description that answers most of the potential tenant's early questions. If they require further details about the property, they can ask you about it. After all, you want them to ring you. It is something of a teaser.

TAKE PICTURES

Don't forget while you are at the property to take several photographs of the house or apartment with your digital camera. The main photograph should be of the front elevation. If it isn't, and you use it on your spec sheets, you must say so. Interior photographs may also be taken if required. Interior photographs can act as an important check at a later date as to the condition and content of the inside of the house. Always ask your landlord's permission if it is in order to photograph the property. It is polite and courteous so to do.

Even if you are not initially instructed, you will have the pictures on file saved for a later date. With the advent of digital cameras you do not have to worry about expensive development costs, so you can go a little mad. In the early days you may like to take twenty or more pics, once you look at them on your computer you can always delete the dodgy ones. By taking a good number of shots you will always find some better ones amongst them. If there is a strong sun shining directly at you, you may need to call back a little later, better that, than poor pics.

With a little ingenuity you will quickly produce neat accurate property spec sheets in full colour using the benefit of modern inexpensive technology. Just because your business is small, new and independent, it does not mean you shouldn't be able to present professional, accurate and competent information. Learn how to email the spec sheets too, as an attachment, together with colour photos. That will impress your landlords and tenants alike. Use modern technology to your advantage. It is an important tool, so use it. If you are not too hot on computers sign up at the local college for a brush-up course.

GOOD SPELLING IS PROFESSIONALISM

Make sure your spelling is up to the mark. You can always enlist the help of the spell checker, though spell checkers are not always to be trusted. My spell checker for example would not recognise the word Liverpool no matter what I did. It consistently wanted to re-write it as Liverwort! Here's a short spelling test. How many of these are incorrectly spelt?

Accomodation
Extention
Tennant
Leese
Negociated
Mezanine
Tennancy
Rentalls
Conservatary
Double-glased
Houseing

Answer: They are <u>ALL</u> INcorrect.
Get it right? Of course you did.

Why is spelling so important anyway? In a word: professionalism. If you can't be bothered to ensure you spell your blurbs correctly, what confidence can the landlord have that you will take the time to prepare your paperwork accurately? Indeed what confidence could they have in anything you do? Some words have a completely different meaning when spelt slightly differently. That could be an important factor on a long tenancy agreement.

Accommodation is the word that property companies spell incorrectly all the time. Make sure you don't. It's easy to remember. Two m's and two c's. That's it.

Make the effort to get it right, check everything and keep improving. Everyone can get better at whatever they do, pay attention to detail; it will eventually be that fact that marks you out from the competition. There's nothing better than to hear a landlord say: "Your paperwork is always so well done!" Excellent. That's the objective. Everything you do is: "So well done". Of course it is!

Ten:
Meeting & Interviewing Prospective Tenants

Meeting and interviewing prospective tenants for the first time can be an interesting experience. It's a fact that absolutely anyone from a member of the Royal family downward may require to rent a home at some stage in their lives. If you have a mental picture of prospective tenants as somehow being downmarket fallen on hard times layabouts, then get rid of the picture. It might have been true once. It certainly isn't now.

Robert Maxwell, when he was alive, rented his mansion from Oxford City Council. He described it as the best council house in all of England. The Duke of Marlborough rents Blenheim Palace from the Crown, albeit for the hefty rental figure of £1 a year on condition they never pay late! Well they wouldn't would they? People who rent property should not be categorised in your mind as any different from people who own their homes, after all, they might be a hundred times wealthier than the people living next door.

Imagine the picture; you have advertised a property, perhaps that two-bedroom first floor flat at 595.00 per month. You receive six calls enquiring about the flat, three of whom would like to view the property.

Try to arrange the viewings at the same time, by same time, I don't mean at precisely the same moment, but say twenty minutes apart, that is usually enough. It doesn't take long to view an unfurnished flat. You could arrange them all at exactly the same time if you really wanted to, or were pushed for time, but I wouldn't recommend it. If you did that, you couldn't give each viewer the individual attention they deserve. Nor could you answer their questions if someone else was bombarding your other ear.

Imagine you booked the viewings for 2pm, 2.20pm and 2.40pm. By block booking it has saved you having to go out a second or even a third time. Arrive early and pick up newspapers and junk mail that will inevitably be littering the hallway. If it's in any way dingy inside, put the lights on, especially in common parts. Lights are always lit in show houses, have you noticed that? And for a good reason, they show off the property to the best advantage. Learn from them. Do what they do, especially if it works.

It's also a very good idea to have some neat business cards printed. When the tenants arrive, hand them a card. It reassures the prospective tenant you are who you say you are. They may also hand the card to someone else later on, if they themselves are not interested in the property. This is a useful source of free advertising.

There's not a great deal to see in an empty flat and I'd recommend you invite them to wander around unaccompanied, as most people prefer to do that. If you feel uncomfortable with it or for some reason uncomfortable with the tenant, you could always show them round but you don't need to announce: "This is the kitchen, this is the bathroom". People are not stupid. On your first couple of viewings you might like to take along someone else with you for moral support.

PERSONAL SECURITY

Here's an important word of warning. Never turn your back on the viewer. Why? Well you have absolutely no idea who they are, or what their history is. Invite them to go on ahead of you, where you can see them. They may have told you that they were a teacher from the local junior school, but at this stage you only have their word for that. The truth is they could be anyone, someone with mental health problems who had recently been returned to the community for example, or an axe murderer, unlikely I agree, but not an impossibility.

Never turn your back on tenants until you learn more about them.

Remember, your security is paramount, and so is your staff's when you begin recruiting. I am sure I don't need to remind you of the dreadful Susan Lamplugh case to illustrate my point as to what could happen, no matter how long the odds against may be, and this applies equally to men as well as women.

Remain vigilant and alert at all times until that person is off the premises. If you can, tell someone where you are going, and what time you will be back. Always take your mobile phone with you, and make sure it is fully charged. Don't take unnecessary risks, however tiny they may seem.

ALWAYS ISSUE AN APPLICATION FORM

When a tenant has finished viewing the property they will almost certainly ask you questions. I always make a point of giving them an application form, whether they are interested in the property or not, together with a sheet of general terms and conditions, including information about the fee payable by them. The point of doing this is, even if they are not interested in that particular property, they will have your letterheads, terms of business, and telephone numbers readily to hand, and they may well ring you back later, or in a day or two.

They might also share an existing property with other potential tenants. They may for example, be residing in a nurse's home where people are coming and going all the time, and if anyone else sees your name and number they might ring you too. It's all about FREE ADVERTISING and PROMOTING YOUR BUSINESS. Getting yourself widely known is not just an expensive newspaper advertising campaign. Word of mouth is, if anything, more important, and far cheaper!

NO SHOWS

Of all the appointments the general public make, you can expect one in five to be a no show. Some people will ring in and cancel, and some will not. If you ring those that didn't bother to show, they will either not answer the telephone, or mumble some feeble excuse. Either way an apology is a rare thing from people like that. All you can do is bite your lip, shrug your shoulders, and think that if they couldn't be bothered to cancel the appointment, what sort of tenant would they have made anyway, especially when it came to honouring rental payments? You are probably better off without them.

Some agents ring all viewers an hour or two prior to the viewing to check if they are going, and you might like to do that too. If it cuts down on the number of no shows and thus reduces the amount of time wasted, it will be time well spent.

COMPLETING & COLLECTING APPLICATION FORMS

Many potential tenants are under pressure to find new accommodation quickly. Perhaps their existing tenancy agreement is rapidly coming to an end and they have been served with a notice to vacate the property. Perhaps they are taking up a new work appointment and need to sort their accommodation prior to that. Perhaps they are being evicted, or repossessed.

Whatever the reason, it is not unusual for keen tenants to fill out an application form there and then, at the viewing, and hand it to you before they leave.

This works well too, because not only can you help them complete the application form accurately and completely, you can also collect the application fee at the same time. Driving away with a completed application form and the accompanying fee of 100.00

or whatever it is, tucked into your pocket serves to inspire you onward to greater things. Remember, this money is yours, it is not the landlords, and it is <u>not</u> returnable. (I'll come back to that in a minute.)

Make sure that on the application form it clearly states that:

<u>Any SECURITY DEPOSIT payable will be returned within 10 days of the tenant vacating the property, by CHEQUE to their new address, providing the rental account is up to date, and the property is returned in good condition.</u>

This is most important and we'll discuss why later in the book.

While you are with the prospective tenant take the opportunity to quiz them about their circumstances and employment. You can often learn as much about someone in five minutes relaxed conversation, as you can from any amount of written information on application forms, or by taking up formal references. You will learn to gain a feel for people. You will often gain an inkling as to whether they are telling fibs. Do tenants tell fibs?

Yes, unfortunately some of them do. Personal intuition can be as good a referencing tool as any number of glowing written references. After ten years experience, I'd back my intuition against written references any day.

While you are with them it's a good idea to picture in your own mind how the letting will pan out three or four months down the line. Imagine for instance, how would it be if this tenant failed to pay the rent. How would you feel about chasing that person? If you thought you might feel in any way intimidated, or that the tenant might in any way be troublesome or difficult to deal with, perhaps a small red warning light should be going off in your mind.

TAKING UP REFERENCES

As soon as you return to the office, start the referencing procedure. Don't put it off till tomorrow, regardless of when the tenant is seeking to start the tenancy, DO IT STRAIGHT AWAY!

It doesn't matter one jot whether you are considering the tenant for one of your own properties or one of your clients, there are five references you should consider taking up.

They are:

1. Employer reference
2. Current landlord reference
3. Previous landlord reference, especially if the current one is for less than a year
4. Banker reference
5. Credit reference

EMPLOYER REFERENCE

The employer's reference is to ascertain whether the applicant is actually employed, and if so, is employed where they say they are. Some employers will tell you a great deal of information about their employees without you ever having to ask for it. Other employers, ever mindful of the data protection act, will tell you almost nothing. Pay particular attention to confirming that the employment is full time. There are many people employed in December who are not in work in January, Post Office sorting workers for example, and professional Santa Clauses.

LANDLORD REFERENCES

The current landlord's reference will ascertain that the applicant lives where they say they live. It may also reveal comments about the applicant's payment history. The previous landlord's reference is the same, and additionally proves the applicant's conduct over a longer period. The landlord's references also serve as a potential introduction for you to new landlords. Don't let this opportunity go to waste. Jot down the landlord's telephone number in your contact book. Don't let them pass you by without at least speaking to them at some point about other property matters.

Be bold; ask them if they have any other property empty or coming empty. Most will tell you if they have.

BANK REFERENCE

The bank reference is the one that most landlords ask about, and yet in my opinion is the one I put the least store by.

In all the time I took up bank references the only statement they ever made was: "Good for normal commitments". What the heck does that mean? One gentleman whom the bank described as: "Good for normal commitments" went bankrupt six weeks after I moved him into an apartment. So how good was that exactly?

I have never seen a detrimental bank reference, ever, and I would question the whole point of carrying one out. Worse still, you have to pay for them these days, and some banks charge as much as 25.00 up front for typing out a brief letter on a single sheet of paper. That is ridiculous! If you decide not to take up bank references and a landlord asks you why you did not, tell them the truth, they are not worth the paper they are written on, they really aren't!

CREDIT REFERENCE

The final reference is the credit reference and this is very important. You will need to sign up with one of the property credit referencing bureaux such as Homelet or Letsure. You'll find their addresses and telephone numbers in the trade directory at the end of this book. If you are not in the UK, simply google Credit Referencing Agencies.

These agencies will of course charge you for the references, normally around 10.00 for a basic report, and up to 25.00 for a comprehensive one. These costs are usually borne by the agent and are paid out of the application fee and that is another very good reason why the application fee should never be returned. Why should you stand the tenant's search fees? Of course you shouldn't. You are a professional business, not a charity. Credit references are usually based on a scoring principle with a pass mark around 140.

I have seen scores well over 300, and as low as 2. The references will show up county court judgments, loan defaults, and similar financial problems in the applicant's background. If a person doesn't have any CCJ's (County Court Judgements) or loan defaults, and is on the current voter's roll, they will almost certainly pass with flying colours.

I always place great faith in credit references. In all my time letting property, I very rarely experienced a financial problem with anyone who had passed a credit reference. I often did, with people who failed. If I had to rely on one reference alone, it would be this one.

Once you've filled out the credit reference application form I recommend you fax or email it to the agency immediately. Speed is of the essence. You cannot rely on snail mail any more. Depending on the service you've signed up for, you can often obtain a reply within the hour, and that might be important.

COMPLETE THE REFERENCING PROCEDURE QUICKLY

Some letting agencies inform their potential tenants, especially the longer established agents, that it takes a week to process an application. Poppycock! Absolute balderdash! Do these people live in the modern age? The fact is that with modern technology, ALL the references can be obtained on the very day the application has been received by the agent, if the agent shows the necessary urgency to obtain them.

Or, if not as quick as that, certainly within twenty-four hours. Remember, it is in your best interest, and your landlord's interest, to process and pass or fail the application as quickly as possible. Why? Because all the while that the proposed deal is up in the air, the tenant has the option of walking away, saying "I've found something better... and cheaper". Just because the potential tenant has applied to you, it doesn't necessarily mean they have stopped looking elsewhere.

You need to know as soon as possible whether the tenant has failed, because if they have, you should be concentrating your efforts on finding someone else. On the other hand if they are a good potential tenant, indeed a very sought after tenant, other agencies might well be in contact with them offering all kinds of attractive rental deals.

This is a competitive world, and good tenants are highly sought after. When you have them in your grasp, don't give them any opportunity to slip away, and don't give your rivals the remotest chance to steal them. If you dilly-dally or prevaricate, that is exactly what will happen.

As a final check you might like to do my 'Me-Me-Me' test. What's the Me-Me-Me test? It's simple. Say to yourself in all honesty, would you be happy to put this person in YOUR house? If the answer is "Yes", all well and good, crack on with it and get the business done, but if the answer is "No", how could you possibly justify putting this person in someone else's house? There's something wrong there somewhere. There could be trouble ahead.

Once you receive an acceptable landlord reference, credit reference, and employer reference, faxed or emailed copies will do, you can speak to your landlord and tell them that you have successfully located a fully referenced tenant, and ask for final permission to proceed. At this stage they may well ask you a few questions about the tenant, such as: "Do they have any pets", or "Are they smokers?"

This may be a way of quickly checking whether you have indeed done your homework properly. If you don't know, don't guess. Tell them you will double check and find out. Most landlords want to let their property as soon as possible, the last thing they need is for a house or flat standing empty, so once you tell them the tenant has passed the referencing procedure, nine times out of ten the landlord will say something like, "Well done, get on with it!"

Another reason to double check with the landlord before you proceed is because they might have instructed other agents to let the same house. I'm sorry to say it often happens that a property that may have been sticking for a week or two suddenly becomes let by two or even three different agencies at the same time, sometimes even to the same bunch of tenants!

Clearly if that's the situation you need to know about it immediately. It's sods law, there's nothing you can do about it, but put it to the back of your mind and concentrate on the next deal.

TENANTS WHO FAIL REFERENCING

What do you do if a tenant fails a reference? All is not yet lost. You need to examine <u>why</u> and by <u>how much</u> they have failed on any particular reference. You must never ignore a failure. You have a duty of care toward the landlord. If you steam ahead and put a tenant into a property knowing full well they have failed their checks, you would be taking a huge risk, and would be storing up big trouble for yourself.

Yes, you may be blinded by the nice fee that you are so close to pocketing, especially if you have experienced a quiet month, but:

NEVER PLACE A TENANT INTO A PROPERTY
WHO HAS FAILED THEIR REFERENCES

Remember, the landlord might ask to see the references at any time, as they are entitled to do. What are you going to say? "Oh I'm sorry I didn't notice it was a failure!" It won't wash, and you could find yourself on the end of a very expensive legal claim, not to mention losing a valued client. Your integrity will have been impugned, and your integrity is something worth guarding. It is something that is easily lost, and something that is almost impossible to recover, once gone.

So what can you do in the event of failure? If the tenant has failed the credit check because of one Court Judgement, perhaps for non-payment of council tax from some years ago, you need to ring the tenant and ask them the full circumstances of the default. If they can't or won't discuss the matter, I would reject them on the spot. If a tenant says they didn't know they had court judgements, you can be fairly sure they are telling fibs. But it isn't difficult to end up with a CCJ; you might be surprised at how many people are wandering around the streets with them. Anyone can forget about occasionally paying a certain bill and end up with a stain on their record. Some utility companies for example are too quick to instigate legal procedures. A whole string of them mind, is a completely different matter.

GUARANTORS

The usual way of proceeding further would be to ask the prospective tenant to provide a GUARANTOR. A guarantor is someone who will sign the tenancy agreement AS WELL as the tenant. They will be responsible for each and every term on that agreement INCLUDING a responsibility to pay the rental, should the tenant ever fail to do so. The guarantor would also be equally responsible for the property to be returned in good condition when the tenancy ends.

It is a big responsibility being a guarantor, and many people will not take it on, unless they have the utmost confidence in the tenant. A guarantor should ideally be employed, and a homeowner. In that case you know if the tenant defaults, the guarantor would have the wherewithal to honour the tenant's obligations.

If a guarantor ever treated the matter as a complete joke by saying something like: "I'll sign anything you want, you won't get a thing from me", and yes, that has happened, reject them immediately.

Reference the guarantor including a credit check, just as you would a tenant. If the guarantor fails the credit check as well, bright red lights should be going off in your mind. Sirens in your head. Guarantors are usually parents, close relatives, or spouses and ex spouses. I would be very suspicious of anyone else standing as a guarantor without good reason. You have to ask yourself, why are they standing as a guarantor? Would you stand as a guarantor for someone you weren't related to or didn't know that well? Unlikely I suspect, for it could hit you hard in the pocket if anything went wrong. Why would you take that risk? Would anyone, unless there was an ulterior motive behind it?

A young lady recently applied for a tenancy on a flat of mine, she failed her credit check by a big margin. She'd viewed the property with her father. I rang him up and asked him if he would stand as a guarantor. He laughed and replied jokily: "No thanks, mate." What does that say? If her own father wouldn't stand as a guarantor, what kind of tenant was she going to make? Needless to say I passed on that one, and I am sure that you would too.

No matter how keen that you, or your landlord is, to fill a particular property, there is always another potential tenant around the corner. If you are struggling to get pass references on a particular tenant, don't be shy to reject them. Even if it's your brother, as once happened to an agent I know! If you populate your properties with borderline tenants, or worse, you will not only gain a reputation for supplying dodgy tenants, but you will be storing up untold problems for yourself in the future.

BAD TENANTS WASTE TIME

Believe me, one bad tenant can take up more of your time than fifty good ones ever will, and they also serve toward taking your eye off the ball, which should be firmly fixed on obtaining and filling more property, not chasing around the wastrels of this world. Remember, the place for wastrels is in the competition's property, not yours.

There is one thing you can certainly rely on, every agency sooner or later will accommodate a bad tenant, it happens to everyone. Perhaps you saw a recent Tenants from Hell programme on the TV where an up market ARLA letting agent put a tenant into a house, a tenant who paid one month's rental and then nothing else, ever again.

The tenant, who it turned out was an experienced defaulter, used every excuse and trick in the book, including issuing a string of rubber cheques, to remain in the property. It was over a year before the agent and the owner finally regained possession of the house. The landlord, a lady who owned just the one property, was forced into selling the house to cover her debts.

So you can see that every agent, no matter how professional, no matter how careful, no matter how diligent, no matter how long established, no matter how many letters they have after their names, can and will house the occasional bad tenant. There are ways and means of dealing with this situation, and we will be covering this later in the book.

For now, the lesson must be, if the references aren't good enough, get a reputable guarantor. If the tenant cannot come up with a good guarantor, reject them, simple as that. The only landlords who may knowingly accept tenants with bad past records are landlords with poor quality run down property.

I have known landlords who really didn't care who was in their property providing they were inhabited. This is all very well, providing you make it clear to those landlords that the tenant had failed their referencing right from the outset. Put it in writing to the landlord, with a little warning, so they can't come back to you at a later date and pretend they didn't know, because they might, if they have the chance.

Some landlords are quite good at shouting the odds, and some landlords have selective memories too. I don't think you will be surprised to learn of that. It's is a human being thing. Putting things in writing is always a good idea. It is solid evidence, if it ever came to that.

HOUSING KNOWN BAD TENANTS IS A TIME BOMB

And one you can do without. But if that is the case, be warned, you may still be storing up great trouble for yourself in the future. The landlord will still expect you to collect the rent on time, and chase up overdue payments if and when the tenant defaults. All this is very time consuming.

If a potential tenant is at any time hostile, difficult, intimidating or disrespectful, in any way toward you, the property, or the landlord, before the let is agreed and before they are issued with the keys, imagine what they could be like after they have moved in. If a tenant is difficult and disrespectful before they move in, at a time when they are supposedly on their best behaviour, a very large warning flashing light should go off in your mind. If a potential tenant were disrespectful to any party prior to completing, I would bin them immediately. Find someone else. And remember, you can ditch a tenant at any point right up until the tenancy is signed and the initial cash paid. After that point, it is an entirely different ball game.

I once had a tenant who passed all his referencing quite comfortably, but during a second final inspection of the property, just prior to signing and paying the cash, he seemed to change in front of my eyes. He became noticeably rude and agitated and aggressive. He started to damage the fitted kitchen, right in front of my eyes. I couldn't believe what I was seeing. He pulled the doors off the hinges, ostensibly to show me how poor condition it was in, he removed the beading, admittedly slightly loose, from all round the worktops.

Inevitably, I saw him in a wholly different light, and I did not like what I was seeing.

I don't know who was the more surprised, the tenant or the landlord, when I cancelled the letting on the spot. I refused to take any money from him and ushered him from the house. He flushed red and bristled like an angry dog. He threatened to sue me for breach of contract, but as I pointed out to him, he didn't have a contract, they were still, thankfully, nestling unsigned in my briefcase.

He flew away from the house, bleating that I hadn't heard the last of it. But I had. I never heard a thing from him again, and fortunately successfully let the property to a lovely music teacher the very next day. A solicitor friend of mine later mentioned that after all that he might have had a case, but I doubt it.

TELL TENANTS THEIR RESULTS QUICKLY

If a potential tenant fails the referencing procedure, you must ring them as soon as you can and advise them that is the case, and that you cannot proceed further. They will probably feign surprise that they have a CCJ, or for whatever reason they have failed, but the fact is, people who have CCJ's almost certainly know full well that they do. They were simply hoping that you wouldn't do your job properly, and discover them.

Some tenants will get hot under the collar and shout at you and demand their fee back. Some tenants will call you names. One tenant, upon being rejected, relieved himself in my hallway. I kid you not, the carpet steamed (and stank!) for ages afterwards. It takes all sorts, and his actions only served to remind me of how right I was not to accept him in the first place. I was just sorry I didn't have the CCTV rigged up at the time. I could have made some money from "You've been framed!"

If your application form stated that the tenant's application fee was non-returnable, then it means precisely that. Don't ever let rejected tenants upset you, or hassle you. You have done the correct thing with a clear conscience, and may have saved your landlord, and yourself, untold problems. Put it out of your mind and concentrate on locating a better tenant for the property, as quickly as you can.

If you receive more than one application for a particular property there is nothing to stop you referencing more than one applicant. You can then select the one who you deem to be the best, and keep the second best in reserve, just in case the first choice doesn't complete.

UNEMPLOYED TENANTS

What do you do if the applicant is unemployed? There are two possible scenarios here. Firstly, the tenant could be paying the rental from private means, in other words they do not need to work. For example we had a lady in her late fifties who required a bungalow for a year. We matched her to a very smart little property on the edge of town at 900.00 per month. She proved she could pay the rent by presenting us with a copy of her bank statement that showed a credit of over a 100,000. We asked her to pay the whole year in advance, which she duly did, 10,800 in cash, of which our commission was 1080.00. Not bad for an afternoon's work.

As you can imagine, the landlord was delighted to receive a cheque the following week for a full year's rent of 9,720.00. He had no idea it was coming. You may be surprised how many tenants will pay rental in advance, if you ask for it; there is no harm in asking, is there? It's another weapon in your armoury. If you have a potential tenant who may not be absolutely top notch, ask them to pay a goodly proportion of rental up front. They can only say no.

The second possibility is that the potential tenant is unemployed and is expecting the State (in Britain, Housing Benefit Office) to pay all, or part of the rental. Housing Benefit is such a wide issue that I have devoted an entire chapter to it a little later in the book.

For now, imagine you have reached the stage where you have located a good employed tenant who has passed the referencing procedure with flying colours; you have the landlord's permission to place the tenant into the property. All that remains is for you to prepare the necessary documentation, collect the cash, and book them in. Progress is being made. Crack on, and complete the deal.

Eleven:
Inventories

An Inventory is a list of the contents within a property. With an unfurnished property there may well not be an inventory at all. Some landlords will prepare their own to include items such as light fittings, carpets, kitchen appliances (if supplied) and the like. As far as any letting agent is concerned, Inventories can be a pain in the neck because they are so time consuming to prepare and check.

The first rule for any agent regarding Inventories is to never promise to produce an Inventory unless it is paid for as an added extra (usually by the landlord). I was stung early in my career when I let a 16 room fully furnished Victorian house. I had previously advertised that I would prepare and check any Inventory for fifty quid. What was I thinking of? The house was crammed from floor to ceiling with eighty years of accrued contents. Never again!

It was furnished from top to bottom down to a packet of cocktail sticks and the landlord took me at my word, and invited me to prepare the inventory. It took me three days! It took all day to check it when the tenant moved in, and all day again, when they moved out. By my arithmetic that was five days work for 50.00. Yeeks!

Worse was to follow because when the tenant eventually moved out there were numerous items missing, though all parties were confident they were there somewhere; it was just that they couldn't be found amid the morass of belongings.

Incredibly, I recently saw an inexpensive property management franchise that was recommending that its franchisees charged their landlords 25.00 to prepare and complete an inventory. In 2008! It makes one wonder if these people have ever actually managed any furnished property, because they clearly have no idea of how much work is involved.

INVENTORIES ARE AN OPPORTUNITY

So if Inventories are a pain in the neck, and so time consuming, how is it that they can also be an opportunity? Because the landlord should pay a realistic additional fee to have them prepared and checked. I guarantee you now that if you quoted say 200.00 for the preparation and checking of an Inventory, a reasonable figure for a large house, almost all landlords would forgo the pleasure. Another alternative is for the landlord to prepare the Inventory themselves. Many do so, especially on furnished properties. They often have an inflated view of what their sticks and stones are worth.

But anyone who has ever invited an auction house to a crammed property to value the chattels will know better what used contents are truly worth. Very little, and that's a fact.

In theory the agent should go through every item, one by one with the tenant to make sure that everything is present and correct. But the truth is that many agents, and I am not just talking about the small agencies either, but many national agents too, present the Inventory to the tenant and ask them to sign it without a check being made. Most tenants do. It is totally unsatisfactory, but the landlord has little ground for complaint, after all they are usually most reluctant to pay anything towards the cost of the preparation and checking.

My advice on Inventories would be quite clear. Advise the landlord it is a chargeable extra from the outset. You can put that in your initial fact pack too so as it won't come as a nasty surprise. If they won't accept it, spend as little time on the duty as you have to. If they are prepared to pay, that's fine, it is another fee for you, to pay for the time that you will undoubtedly spend on the chore. Remember, you are a professional person, running a professional agency, and you should expect to be paid for your time. There's nothing in this world for free. Never work for nothing. Your local long established agency, your competitor, certainly won't.

When the tenant moves out and the Inventory is checked again, it will no doubt reveal a shortage of a varying degree of items. Most landlords are fair and reasonable, but some are not. Making a claim against the security deposit should in theory pay for the items that are missing or damaged, but of course the tenant may dispute your findings. Occasionally you will come across a landlord who sticks to this to the letter.

For example, one landlord I worked for wanted to claim for a missing yellow pages telephone directory, (they are FREE!), half a bar of soap that had long since been used up, one dead light bulb, and a used and missing Hoover bag! The rental on the property was 1,250.00 per month and had been paid impeccably. Talk about Scrooge! The tenant was from overseas. I hate to imagine what impression he took home with him.

Always remain cheerful and calm, smooth things over, rise above any hassle, and leave at the first opportunity. Oh, and by the way, the best thing any agent can do to smooth over heavy waves that inventory checks may throw up, is to let the property again, and as quickly as possible, to a fresh tenant in order to start the rental payments flowing again. Fat rental cheques have a magic way of making minor disputes evaporate in thin air.

Twelve:
Signing Contracts
& Booking Tenants
In To Property

It goes without saying that the preparation of the legal tenancy agreement is one of the most important duties any letting agent has to accomplish. Quite simply it has to be done right. Errors can be very costly, as we have already seen. Great care should be taken over it, and they should be thoroughly checked, and checked again. This is especially true when you first start letting property.

However, once a procedure has been established, providing it is followed rigorously, things will improve. It is like so many things in life, once you have completed one successfully, it is so much easier to do thereafter.

CHOOSING THE TENANCY AGREEMENT

There are four likely tenancy agreements that you may consider using. They are:

1. The Oyez printed tenancy agreement from the Law Society
2. A computerised tenancy agreement within purchased or leased software

3. The landlord's own tenancy agreement
4. Your own custom designed agreement

All of these tenancy documents in the UK should be Assured Shorthold Tenancy Agreements. For residential property I highly recommend that you stick with the Assured Shorthold and you won't go far wrong.

The first one, the Oyez, is available from the Law Society and you will need two copies for each let. One is known as the "party" and the other the "counter party". The landlord retains one, and the tenant the other.

Note that with Oyez there is a slightly different form for furnished property as opposed to unfurnished. If you are using the Oyez contract, it is a good idea to keep a stock in hand of say 10 of each; readily available in case you need some in a hurry.

The benefits of the Oyez contract is that they are spot on, legally speaking, and look the part, but the downside of that contract is that for many landlords nowadays they are simply nowhere near comprehensive enough when it comes to all the do's and don'ts with regard to their precious property.

The second one, the tenancy agreement within a software package is becoming more the norm. The advantages are that you can print off as many as you like without extra charge, and let as many properties as you wish, and you never need to buy forms as such, although of course the software itself does need to be purchased or leased. You also never run out. The computerised contracts are all embracing running to perhaps six or seven pages with many clauses that the tenant needs to agree to. You can also easily add additional clauses if necessary, as some landlords may request, or delete certain other clauses if they are obviously incompatible or unacceptable to a particular let. There are not many drawbacks to this type of contract, except perhaps the sheer length of them.

USE A LANDLORD'S AGREEMENT AT YOUR PERIL

The third tenancy agreement you may have to consider using is the landlord's own tenancy agreement. This can be a very dangerous option, and you should tread very warily in that direction. I have seen numerous tenancy agreements prepared by landlords that are frankly not worth the paper they are written on. Some are blatant slightly amended copies of other copyrighted documents, some include clauses that are blatantly illegal, and some are obviously legally flawed.

If you prepared a tenancy agreement using a flawed landlord's form, and subsequently there was a problem, the landlord might still have a case against you. Their argument might be: "You're the agent, the supposed expert, you should have advised me differently".

I would be very reluctant to use a landlord's own agreement and in all my time as an agent I only ever did so twice. I rejected numerous such agreements as being quite unacceptable, and most landlords were happy enough to use our agreements once they had inspected them.

To give two examples of what a landlord had included in their own agreements, the first lady had written in that on leaving the property the tenant would return, and at the tenant's expense, fully decorate the property from top to bottom.

In my experience that would be quite unworkable. Firstly, most tenants would baulk at that to begin with, resulting in many lost lets, and secondly, I could not imagine any tenant actually carrying out the work, resulting in numerous heated telephone calls, and much wasted time.

Another gentleman had written his own agreement in block capital letters. His spelling was atrocious and it included the clause that the tenant must leave the property at any time during the tenancy within 7 days should the landlord so demand.

This was blatantly illegal too, quite contrary the terms of an Assured Shorthold Agreement and the Housing Act. I refused point blank to have anything to do with it, and the landlord pressed ahead regardless and installed a tenant who foolishly signed the agreement put before him. The last I heard, the landlord was being investigated and subsequently prosecuted by the local housing authority for harassing his tenants, and worse.

If you have a landlord who absolutely insists on using their own agreement, ask your solicitor or lawyer to view it. If the solicitor objected to it in any way, I wouldn't touch it with a barge pole. Find someone else, another landlord with sensible and acceptable documentation.

PREPARING YOUR OWN AGREEMENT FORM

The last choice would be an agreement you may be tempted to prepare from scratch yourself. The advantages of this would be that you could include whatever clauses you think were appropriate, and you would never have to pay a penny for it. However the great disadvantage is that you run the very real risk that you could produce a document that is not legally binding.

It may look OK to you, but are you legally qualified to know? Did you know for example that the size of margins on an agreement is supposed to be of a certain dimension? On that technicality alone, a judge could set aside an agreement, in the case of a dispute.

How would you care to ring a landlord and explain that you couldn't get a tenant out of their property, because the agreement you had produced, had been set aside by a judge as being illegal. It doesn't bear thinking about.

If you are tempted to set up your own contract, and I can see that after you gain some experience, you might be, you absolutely <u>must</u> have it inspected and passed by a solicitor. And don't forget that you must not copy, word for word, other agreements that you may have come across. They are invariably copyrighted documents, and you would be committing an offence if you did so. The penalties for breaching copyright are rightly harsh. Don't take the risk. It can also look cheap, and we are never cheap.

This might sound heavy, but you can appreciate that a legally binding contract simply has to be prepared absolutely correctly. To muck around with something you do not truly understand could be a recipe for disaster. I used the Oyez contracts for many years, before switching to a computerised product within a software package. I can honestly say that in all that time, during which we prepared thousands of agreements, we never had a serious problem with regard to an incorrectly completed agreement.

My advice would be, once you have prepared your first agreement, have your solicitor cast their eye over it before it is presented to the landlord or tenant for their signature. Once you've completed one successfully, you will rapidly gain confidence in preparing countless others thereafter. Your solicitor will point out any potential errors in your work, and remember, they are fully qualified to do so.

Once your tenancy documentation is up to the mark, and duly prepared for your first agreed let, it is time to look at the occasionally fractious business of tenants' deposits.

TENANTS' DEPOSITS

Almost all landlords require a security deposit to be paid along with the first month's rental. This deposit is more often than not the equivalent of an additional month's rent. Some agents and some landlords too, are nowadays seeking more than one month's rent as a deposit, perhaps a month and a half, or a month plus 150.00, or even two months.

Your market research will have told you what your local competitors are doing with regard to this.

You can ask for any amount of security deposit you want; but do remember that once you ask for more than a month's rent as a deposit, you will dramatically reduce the number of applications you will receive for any particular property.

Many tenants will baulk at paying more than a month as a deposit. Remember, this is on top of the first month's rent. Take a detached house for example that could be on your books for 850.00 per month. If the tenant needed to pay 850.00 first month's rent, plus another 850.00 deposit, plus your processing fee of say 100.00., they would need to find 1,800.00 in cash before they could contemplate moving in. For many people that is a hefty sum. But if you then increased the deposit again to say a month and half, that same tenant would need to find a whopping 2,225.00.

There are many people out there with that kind of money readily available, but equally, there are many well-qualified employed people who simply don't have that kind of ready cash sitting about. Does the landlord really want to pass up on an otherwise excellent tenant in full time employment because they can't or won't stump up an additional deposit?

In my experience most landlords would hugely prefer to have the house let, to have that tenant in the property, as would I if it were mine, every time.

To some extent you need to liase with the landlord on the matter of deposits. Some will tell you their terms with regard to deposits and will never budge an inch; while others will take your advice. If it was my house and it was empty, and the tenant had passed all their references, and was paying a full month's deposit, I would always accept them, and start the rental flowing.

An empty property is a liability. It could be another three months before you locate someone else who was prepared to pay that extra deposit. If it stayed empty for three extra months, (quite feasible) that would be a loss of rental on that property alone of 2,550.00, a big financial loss that could never be recovered, no matter how soon afterwards it was let, and all because of a relatively small additional deposit. You have to be realistic. So does the landlord. Sometimes you have to impress that upon them. A let house is a profitable house. An empty house is dead money.

What happens to the deposit? A very good question. Prior to April 2007 the letting agent could simply keep it, place it on deposit and earn and pocket the interest earned. In Britain today, that is no longer the case.

TENANCY DEPOSIT PROTECTION SCHEMES

All deposits now taken on assured shorthold tenancies (for rent up to 25,000 per annum) by landlords and letting agents in England and Wales now have to be protected by an authorised deposit scheme.

To avoid disputes going to court each scheme is supported by a dispute resolution service whose aim is to make disputes over the repayment of deposits faster and cheaper to resolve.

In the first year alone in the UK almost a billion pounds of tenants' money was safeguarded in this way because landlords and letting agents now have a legal duty to sign up to one of three Government backed schemes when they take deposits. Here's an interesting stat. In Britain the average deposit on Shortholds is now almost £1,000.

You must be aware that any landlord or letting agent who does not sign up for such a scheme is committing a civil offence which could result in them having to pay tenants three times the value of the deposits, but worse still, if that is not bad enough, the landlord could forfeit their right to the possession of their property. Ouch!

SO WHAT ARE THESE DEPOSIT SCHEMES?

DPS – The Deposit Protection Service. This is a custodial scheme where landlords and agent must hand over the deposit in full. It is free to use and open to all letting agents and landlords. The DPS service is entirely funded from the interest earned on deposits held. If a dispute arises between the landlord and tenant at the end of the tenancy the scheme will hold the amount until the dispute resolution service or courts decide the outcome.

TDSL – The Tenancy Deposit Solutions Ltd is a partnership between the National Landlords Association and Hamilton Fraser Insurance. This insurance based tenancy deposit protection scheme enables landlords, either directly, or indirectly through agents to hold deposits.

TDS – The Tenancy Deposit Scheme is another insurance backed deposit and protection and dispute resolution service run by The Dispute Service that builds on a scheme that was originally established in 2003 to provide dispute and resolution and complaints handling from the lettings industry. This also enables landlords and agents to hold deposits.

On the TDSL and TDS the landlord or letting agent has to pay an insurance fee to be covered.

All the Deposit money is held by the schemes until it is time to be repaid at the end of the letting.

<u>THE LANDLORD OR AGENT MUST INFORM THE TENANT WITHIN 14 DAYS OF TAKING THE DEPOSIT THE DETAILS OF HOW THE DEPOSIT IS BEING PROTECTED</u>

You must not forget to do that. At the end of the tenancy the property should be checked over and the landlord or agent should agree with the tenant of how much of the deposit should be returned to them. The agreed amount must be returned to the tenant within 10 days.

In cases where no agreement can be reached about how much of the deposit should be returned, there will be a FREE service to help resolve disputes offered by the scheme that is protecting the deposit.

These schemes are still in their infancy and amendments and updates are bound to come thick and fast. Check out www.direct.gov.uk/en/TenancyDeposit for the latest and additional information.

Remember this: There are some tenants out there who are very worldly wise when it comes to renting properties. Some of them will know the rules and regs as well as you do. As a government spokesperson recently said: "Some landlords and some agents could be in for a very rude shock as tenancies come to an end."

It is up to you to make sure that you are never included in that. Go to school on all the information available on tenants' deposit protection, and there is lots of it, and you will never go far wrong. Keep abreast of it, become an expert on it and if you do, landlords will seek you out to ask your advice and pick your brains. There is nothing wrong in that. You are going to be the best-informed letting agent in your town, in your county. It is only to be expected.

The only people who will lose out because of this new legislation are the unscrupulous landlords, some of whom used the deposit pool to pillage with unjustifiable claims, and some of whom, it has to be said, gave the whole industry a terrible name, by almost never returning deposits.

As far as the letting agent is concerned, this is a good scheme, because in the past, some landlords put pressure on letting agents by saying something like, "You get me half of that deposit or you will lose the property." Now the ultimate decision has been taken from the agents and landlords' hands, and that fractious arguing over what deductions were to be made is no longer decided in the letting agents' offices. I know several agencies that are very happy with that.

FINALISING CONTRACTS

Your contracts are ready to be signed. It makes no difference whether the landlord or the tenant signs first. If you have a quiet afternoon pop round and see the landlord and get them to sign.

Don't be tempted to send contracts through the post if you can avoid it, and <u>NEVER</u> send contracts to tenants through the post. If you did that, you would have no idea who had actually signed the agreement; and that could be important at a later date.

Once the landlord has signed the tenancy agreement and you have the forms back, they cannot change their mind, or rent the property to someone else at more money, or give it to another agent, or sell it with vacant possession, or move a family member into the house, all very good reasons to have them sign as quickly as possible.

You should also make it quite clear to the tenant that you must have CLEARED FUNDS before you would be able to release the keys. In other words if the tenant is meeting you to sign at the house, and pay on the day the contract is due to start, the tenant MUST PAY IN CASH, or by banker's draft, for ALL the monies due.

DO NOT under any circumstances at this late stage accept a personal cheque for either the rental OR the deposit. If the tenant does not pay with cleared funds,

DO NOT RELEASE THE KEY. Sob stories about having nowhere else to sleep are irrelevant. The tenant clearly knew that cleared funds were required. It should say so on your application form. If they can't, or won't produce the cash, it may mean their personal cheque might bounce. It could mean they don't possess the money at all. Take them to the bank if need be, but get the cash.

One way of avoiding last minute hassles is to arrange to meet the tenant a week or more before the contract starts, either at your office, or the tenant's existing house, or at the property they are renting, but do make absolutely sure that you allow enough time for personal cheques to clear.

It takes longer than you think for cheques to clear. It takes longer than three days, regardless of what anyone says. Clearing banks will sometimes bounce cheques up to 8 days after presentation, and there is nothing you can do about it when they do. You might consider EXPRESS CLEARING cheques, though that involves an expense that should really be paid for by the tenant, especially if they have caused the delay, but you try getting it. It won't be easy.

One thing is crystal clear, it would be totally disastrous, as I am sure you can imagine, to receive a letter from the bank a day or two _after_ the tenant has moved into a property, stating that their cheque has bounced.

If you have any doubt:
DON'T RELEASE THE KEYS UNTIL YOU ARE CERTAIN
That ALL funds have cleared.

ARRANGING ONGOING PAYMENTS

You will need to give the tenant a receipt for all monies received. If you know which scheme the deposit is heading for, you can advise them of that now. Perhaps you could prepare a standard letter to give out covering this point.

You can also advise the tenant at this time about ongoing maintenance problems procedures, as to whether they should contact the landlord direct, or liase with you.

If you are managing the property on an ongoing basis you will need to make arrangements to collect future rental payments, and far and away the best method of doing this is by Standing Order Mandate. You can obtain a typical standing order mandate form from your bank, or you can design your own on your PC.

Suggest to ALL tenants they pay by Standing Order Mandate, indeed some agents and landlords insist on payment by SOM and will not entertain tenants unless they agree to this. If they are reluctant to agree, you might ask yourself, why?

If a tenant says, "I'm not paying by Direct Debit because you might take whatever you like from my account", take the opportunity to politely correct them. A Standing Order Mandate is NOT the same thing as a direct debit. A Standing Order Mandate is **always** in the control of the account holder, the tenant, unlike a direct debit. Only the account holder can start and stop

Standing Order Mandate payments, and only they can amend the amounts paid.

If the tenancy started on the 15th of October and they have paid the first month's rent along with the deposit, the next rental payment is obviously due on November 15th. The Standing Order Mandate therefore should state "Please pay 800.00 (or whatever the figure is) on the fifteen of November to Brent's Rents and on the fifteenth of each month thereafter until cancelled by me".

Once the tenant has signed the SOM take a photocopy of it for your records, and then mail or deliver by hand, it must be the <u>original,</u> by first class post to the tenant's bank. Put a note in your diary when the next payment is due to appear and check the bank account daily to monitor what payments are in, and just as importantly, what payments are not.

<u>SET UP ONLINE BANKING</u>

If you haven't done so already, we strongly advise you instigate online banking procedures. That way you can check two or three times a day, if need be, from your own office, and it saves having to ring the bank when you will almost certainly be put on hold more often as not. I don't know about you but those PRESS 3 type of automated answering machines are one of the banes of my life! As for eventually getting through to someone on the other side of the planet who can barely speak English, well that type of dreadful service beggars belief. Thankfully some of the banks have finally cottoned on to the fact that business people will not accept such dire service indefinitely, though other banks still have a way to go

If the tenant will not agree to a Standing Order Mandate facility being set up, perhaps it is because there is no money in their bank account, in which case another warning light should start flashing. One way of insisting a tenant pays by Standing Order, is to state as much before the let is finally agreed.

You do not need to make a big issue of it; you can simply say, the landlord requires the rent to be paid by Standing Order Mandate directly to us. Okay? If they don't agree, why don't they? In my experience good tenants always agree. They don't want to have to bother about remembering and writing out and posting off cheques every month, anymore than you do.

AVOID HAVING TO COLLECT RENTS IN PERSON

Nevertheless, despite your best efforts, some tenants, even if they agree to pay by SOM initially, will not do so for long. The alternatives are for them to drop cheques, and or cash, into your office, but whatever you do, don't be railroaded into chasing them round collecting the rent. That is not your responsibility. It is the tenant's responsibility to deliver the rent to your office, or preferably, to your bank account. Chasing round after difficult people is a massive time waster. Avoid it.

Always retain the initiative, set the rules yourself. If the tenant doesn't like them they can always go elsewhere. Put the onus on them to deliver. You can be sure the big established agencies in your town will do exactly the same. If the tenant smells a weakness in your resolve, they may well start playing games with you, such as, "Can you come and collect the rent at 7pm?" You go in the rain, in the snow, and they're not in. They might think it is funny. You most certainly will not, and neither will the landlord. If there was more than one incidence of that, I would write them a straight letter reminding them of their responsibilities.

BOOKING TENANTS IN

Once the tenant has paid all of the upfront money and the funds are cleared, and once both parties have signed the agreement, you can release their copy of the tenancy agreement, and arrange to book them into the property. The landlord's copy can be sent to him or her, together with their first statement of account and payment.

When you book the tenant into the property you must **always** attend. Never pass the key to the tenant in your office and wish them luck. ALWAYS arrange to meet them at the property. While you are there you should make a note of the gas and electricity meter readings and have the tenant sign your booking in slip to confirm the figures. Water too, if there is a water meter. The tenant should also sign for the quantity of keys you are issuing.

Go round the property with the tenant and make a note of any obvious damage or noticeable wear and tear at the property. For example, the lounge carpet may be badly stained. Note the fact. Photograph it too, if you think it will show up in your pic. Perhaps a small pane in the glazed front door may be cracked, again note the fact on your file. The reason for recording imperfections such as this is because at the end of the contract, if the landlord attempts to make a claim against the deposit, you can refer to your notes, and photographs, and say: "Sorry but that was like that before the tenant moved in".

Take the opportunity to have the tenant sign the Inventory too, if one is supplied, or has been prepared by you or the landlord. It should be in duplicate in order that the tenant can keep one copy, and you can retain the other. The Inventory can and often is attached to the tenancy agreement itself, and forms part of the contract.

In my experience no matter how many things you may check in the property on the day the tenancy starts, it is quite impossible to categorically say whether everything in the house is working perfectly or not. It is not until someone actually moves into a house that minor problems might appear. For example you wouldn't know if the central heating started banging loudly after it had been on for twenty minutes, or that the immersion heater cuts out after ten.

Thus, I always said to every tenant, "If there's anything else that shows up in the next day or so please let us know". That way you can list any defects on the file and report them to the landlord. You won't hear a word from most tenants again, while some, at the opposite end of the spectrum, will pester you with a huge list of the most minor defects. There is nothing wrong in that, at least you now know about it, and it is on the record.

You have read the meters and checked the property over, the tenant has signed and paid, and has been issued with their copy of the agreement. There only remain a couple of duties to perform before you can get away. It's always a very good idea to ask the tenant to go outside, close the front door, and re-enter the property using the keys you have just issued. This not only ensures the keys are the right ones, but with so many unusual locks around these days, it saves you the possibility of having to return at a later hour to demonstrate how to lock and unlock doors. It happens believe me, and quite a lot. Tilt and slide conservatory doors can be a real nuisance in this respect. Some people never seem to get the hang of them.

Finally you can expect the tenant to ask you, especially if it is winter, how to use the central heating. This can be a pain too, as many systems differ. If they ask you to demonstrate, it's very difficult to refuse, so a little earlier practice may well pay dividends, and it will also check that the heating is actually working.

REPORT THE METER READINGS

When you have finished your tasks at the property, return to the office and write to the utility companies. (Gas, Water, Electric, and Council Tax). Advise them that the tenant moved into the property on the 15th of May (or whatever date) confirm the meter readings you took. The reason for these letters is that once you've advised the service suppliers of a new tenant being installed, all new bills will then automatically be sent directly to the tenant. Your landlord, or yourself, if the house belongs to you, are then clear of any responsibility for those services. Clearly this would not apply if the rental charged included the cost of some of those services.

Even if the absolute worst came to pass and the tenant never paid a penny to any of the utility companies, the utility suppliers cannot then turn to you, or the property owner, and say: "It's your house, you pay the outstanding £1,000 electricity bill", providing:

a) A proper tenancy agreement was in force, and
b) You have written to them and advised them that the tenant was now in residence.

If there is no legitimate tenancy agreement in existence the owner of the house could still be responsible for all bills. Make sure you never fall into that particular trap. It is also one more good reason to ensure that amateur landlords have a proper tenancy agreement in place.

Lastly, you might like to ring the landlord, for public relations purposes, and say: "The tenant's now booked into the house, everything went well, and you'll receive a payment within 7 days", or whatever you have previously agreed. It also gives you the opportunity to mention, "Oh by the way there is a loose slate or two at the front", or anything else that came up during your visit and inspection.

Be upbeat about it, you should be, for you have successfully let the property in the face of fierce competition from all the other companies that traipse over your beat. They didn't do it, you did! Be brave and ask the landlord: "Have you anything else to rent? I've another really nice person looking".

They will soon tell you if they have, and they'll remember you too, if another of their houses suddenly becomes empty. There will be times when you have to ring landlords with bad news, so make the most of it when you are calling them with good.

DON'T FORGET TO:

Set up Standing Order Mandates
Arrange online banking facilities
Note all meter readings
Write to the Utility companies
Arrange for tenants to sign inventories
Note and photograph property
imperfections

Thirteen:
Statements & Accounting

When you start your property management business you should make sure you open two distinct and quite separate business bank accounts, namely:

<u>Your Current Account:</u>
This contains YOUR money paying YOUR bills

<u>Clients' Account:</u>
This contains the clients' rental monies, and does NOT belong to you

Start as you mean to go on. These two accounts are entirely separate and should NEVER be confused or intermingled.

NEVER pay any of <u>your</u> bills from the clients' account. This would be tantamount to stealing. You would be using other peoples' cash for your own purposes.

As we have previously detailed, tenants' deposits must now be handled in a secure and approved way. Never do anything outside of the laid down systems or you will come a mighty cropper.

At the time of writing there is still no regulation in force within the UK where a regulatory body can come to your office and demand to inspect your clients' account balances. I expect that to change. If and when it does, your books must be absolutely spot on. Don't give anyone, regulatory or not, any opportunity to suggest otherwise. If you have any doubt at all about the way you are handling and accounting with clients' monies, speak to your qualified accountant and they will immediately set you straight.

Woe betide any agent or landlord who experienced a spot check, and was found to have dipped into, or muddled up the clients' money, or worse still, had spent it. It happens. Prosecution would unquestionably follow. Be warned. Clients' money is precisely that. Abuse it at your peril.

Get it right from the start, keep it right, and have it rigorously audited by an independent auditor or accountant at least once a year. If you adhere to these simple rules you won't go far wrong, and you shouldn't have a problem.

When you receive the rental payments, ALL rental payments should be banked directly into the Clients' account using the appropriate pay in book or directed there by your Standing Order Mandates. Thus all your mandate forms should bear only the clients' account bank details. Make sure this clients' account is an interest bearing one. The interest accrued is yours, and can add up to a decent additional revenue stream.

BANK ALL MONIES QUICKLY

Always bank money as quickly as you can. Try not to leave money unbanked overnight, and never leave cash and cheques lying around in your house or office where an opportunistic sneak thief might stumble on it. Bank every day.

Remember, if you received a thousand pounds in rent and a thousand pounds deposit from a tenant, and then lost it, you would have to make it good out of your own pocket (notwithstanding any insurance policies that might assist you). This would be an expensive, but easy mistake to make.

With all this cash sloshing through your accounts your bank manager will think you are wonderful, and it won't be long before he or she is inviting you to lunch, mark my words, they do, and doesn't that make a pleasant change to the usual calls bank managers make? In times of low interest rates the interest accrued is nothing special. But in times of high interest levels, you will be very pleased to see your quarterly bank statement, and the extra revenue that has accrued.

PREPARING LANDLORDS' STATEMENTS

Once you have banked the cash, you should prepare the landlord's statement. Different software packages produce differing styles of invoices, but they should show the following basic details:

- Landlord's name and address with post or zip code, so you can use window envelopes. They save a great deal of time addressing letters
- The tenant's name
- The date and amount of rental collected

- Details of the deposit paid and where it is going
- Any deductions, such as insurance premiums, repairs that you may have organised, or inventory compilation
- Your fees and commission, which should be deducted from the gross amount received

To take a simple example, imagine you have let a flat at 500.00 pcm, and you are managing the property. Your standard fee is 100.00 on each let plus 10% of the collected rental. There were no insurance deductions or repairs. The arithmetic would look like this.

Deposit received, paid into scheme A: <u>500.00</u>

Rent received	500.00
Landlords Fee 100.00	
10% commission 50.00	
<u>Total deductions</u>	<u>150.00</u>
<u>Balance Due to Landlord</u>	<u>350.00</u>

There is no VAT shown because you are **not** yet VAT registered. If you were, your fees would be liable for VAT too, currently running at a rate of 17.5%. VAT is not currently chargeable on residential rentals

PREPARING THE LANDLORD'S PAYMENT

A payment may then be prepared from the clients' account for the landlord. There are two recommended methods of paying landlords, by cheque or direct bank transfer. Never get involved in dishing out cash to landlords, not only is this a security risk, it is most unprofessional. And if you do it once, I guarantee the landlord will be forever hovering around outside your office, waiting for their next whack of cash. Don't go there. Ever.

I greatly favour the direct bank transfer payment method for four good reasons.

1. It is much cheaper as far as bank charges are concerned
2. The payment cannot be lost in the post or mislaid
3. The money hits the landlord's account quickly and is easily trackable and traceable
4. There is far less clerical work involved

In saying that, there are still many landlords who prefer for their own reasons to see a cheque accompanying their monthly statement, and that is their prerogative.

Never become involved with using the landlord's money, at the landlord's request, to pay a third party not known to you, or paying their mortgage direct. That could cause fearful problems. For example, they may notice at a later date when their accounts were being audited, that they did not receive from you a rental payment in March, but they may forget that they asked you to pay someone else for some other service. You might forget too, and pay the landlord again, in effect for a second time. Always pay the landlord's money, to the landlord, and no one else.

If you agreed to pay their mortgage directly and for some reason a payment went missing, imagine the landlord's fury if they received a written warning letter from the building society or bank, possibly even threatening re-possession. It's a potential pitfall you want nothing to do with.

Save the statement on your computer, and when the next month's payment comes round, you can simply adjust the dates, saving a lot of work again. Don't forget though to remove the one off 100.00 fee, so the next month's balance to the landlord, on that particular let, again assuming no additional deductions, would be 450.00.

Where you are not managing a property and the pre agreed fee is half a month's rental, your arithmetic would look like this.

Deposit received and paid into scheme A: <u>500.00</u>
Rent received   500.00
<u>Landlords Fee   250.00-</u>
<u>Balance due to Landlord: 250.00</u>

Make sure both the landlord and tenant are aware of where the deposit has been paid to, whichever scheme you have arranged for your lettings' deposits.

If the landlord had instructed you to set up an insurance policy or do any additional other work, such as a gas safety check, now is the time to make sure the cost is deducted, because unlike a full management contract, you will have no further funds to deduct the expenses from in the future. If you have to slightly delay paying the landlord here, then so be it. Print out hard copies for yourself as a permanent record, and save all statements on your computer.

Once the statement of account is finalised you can proceed to preparing and authorising the payment, again from the clients' account.

TOTALLING YOUR OWN FEES

At the end of each month you should tot up the total fees charged to your landlords. These fees are now your money.

Imagine you had twenty-three landlords' invoices in the month, seventeen of which produced 60.00 fees, three producing 275.00, and three producing 250.00, your total fees billed for that month would be 2,595.00.
That is:

$$17 \times 60 = 1020$$
$$3 \times 275 = 825$$
$$\underline{3 \times 250 = 750}$$
$$\underline{Total \quad 2,595}$$

This figure can now be transferred from the clients' account to your business's current account, on the first day of the month. A summary justifying the payment should be prepared and kept on file. If there has been any interest received, (interest is usually credited quarterly and tax is normally deducted before the money is paid to you by your bank), then you can add that to the summary too. One month in three there should be interest for you, and that can be transferred out of the clients' account at the same time. Don't think these figures are over egging the cake. It should be perfectly possible to let 50 properties in your first year and at least that many in your second, so your total monthly income should increase month on month.

If you have any doubts about whether you are dealing correctly with the payments and transfers from the clients' account do not hesitate to discuss it with your accountant. They will immediately set you right if you are making mistakes. Remember, it is far better to put mistakes right in the first month, rather than at a later date. Monthly mistakes carried over can mount up very quickly, and you don't want to be facing a huge refund back to the clients' account.

One final point, if you buy or lease specialised property management software to look after your statements, it will do much of this work for you, including all the arithmetical calculations. If you want my advice, get some. It will give your business a more professional image, cachet, if you prefer, and your systems will forever be automatically updated as times and procedures inevitably evolve.

To recap:

Open the correct bank accounts
Never leave money lying about
Bank Money Quickly
Prepare landlords' statements
Action landlord payments
Prepare monthly summary of fees earned
Pay yourself the balance of the summary
Keep on top of all accounting

Fourteen:
The Riddle that is
Housing Benefit

There is no topic or aspect of property letting and management that is guaranteed to stir up the blood in Britain as much as the riddle that is Housing Benefit. It doesn't matter whether you are renting three or four properties of your own, or are managing six hundred properties, as a successful property agency, the subject of Housing Benefit will rear its head.

You have two stark choices. You either become an expert on it, or you ignore it. That is for you to decide. For my part I will try and put across the benefits (sorry to use that word again) and problems that this animal can produce.

It is true there are more myths and legends about Housing Benefit than just about anything else in the property world. I'm sure you will have heard of many of them before. Something along these lines:

1. Housing Benefit is guaranteed
2. The Agent collects the Benefit direct; the tenant can't then redirect it
3. Housing Benefit cannot be reclaimed by the Benefit office

4. Housing Benefit will pay the entire contracted rental
5. Housing Benefit will come through straight away
6. The Housing Benefit office is easy to deal with
7. Everyone is entitled to Housing Benefit
8. The Letting Agent is responsible for sorting out the Benefit
9. The Housing Benefit will automatically increase every year
10. Housing Benefit is easy

Ladies and gentlemen, I am sure you won't be surprised to learn that ALL of those statements are incorrect, and yet they are often trotted out, and many more besides. They sometimes lead to the ready-made excuses that some Housing Benefit tenants dream up, such as:

1. I can't pay the rent this month because the Benefit has not come through, or
2. I can't pay the rent this month because the giro's lost in the post and even:
3. I can't pay the rent this month because the Benefit Office is on strike.

Where do you start? And why bother? Well perhaps surprisingly there are good reasons to bother, so let's start at the top and look at those ten initial statements.

HOUSING BENEFIT IS GUARANTEED

It is NOT. It never has been and never will be. Each person is assessed for Housing Benefit on their individual merits. Some qualify, some don't.

THE AGENT COLLECTS THE BENEFIT DIRECT

Many agents do collect benefit directly into their clients' bank account, and there are good and bad reasons for doing so, but a tenant can at any time go into the Benefit office and redirect those benefits back to themselves with one simple letter. It is THEIR benefit, and although they sign a letter stating that it will be spent on rental payments ONLY, in many cases, it isn't.

PAID BENEFIT CANNOT BE RECLAIMED

Nonsense. Oh yes it can! A friend of mine, an elderly landlady had a tenant in a property for three years and in all that time the Benefit office paid the entire rental totalling just over £9,000. The tenant then disappeared and the following month, the landlady received a letter from the Council requesting that ALL that money be returned, as the tenant had claimed it illegally. The landlady is still fighting the case through the courts, and I wish her well.

HOUSING BENEFIT WILL PAY ALL THE RENT

Rubbish! They have restrictions and guidelines to decide how much they may contribute. They might pay it all, they might not. They might not pay any of it.

HOUSING BENEFIT COMES THROUGH STRAIGHT AWAY

Oh, I wish! In one fairly recent case it took Liverpool City Council seven months before payments commenced. I'm sure they would say differently, but it seemed to me they were deliberately obstructing payments at every turn. They couldn't possibly have been doing that, could they? A local authority trying to save cash?

THE HOUSING BENEFIT OFFICE IS
IS EASY TO DEAL WITH

Some offices are better than others. I sympathise with anyone who works on the front desk in any Housing Benefit office. They are rushed off their feet, tempers fray, and verbal abuse is a common occurrence. Physical abuse isn't unheard of either. I'd want a premier league footballer's pay to take that job. You won't be surprised to learn that their staff don't appear to hang around too long.

EVERYONE IS ENTITLED TO HOUSING BENEFIT

Once again that is gibberish! I am not for a start, and I doubt if you are either. Most asylum seekers don't qualify either, and that fact may surprise a few.

THE LETTING AGENT IS RESPONSIBLE FOR
SORTING OUT THE HB

What a laugh! They certainly are NOT! Some lazy tenants may tell you that. You tell them to get of their backsides and go and get the matter sorted. It is THEIR benefit and it is THEIR responsibility to sort it out.

HOUSING BENEFIT AUTOMATICALLY INCREASES

Nope is doesn't. You can apply for an increase annually, but there is no certainty you will receive anything. In one recent case the increase my most successful landlord received was 12 pence per week! It didn't even pay for the stamp on the application.

So after that litany you might be forgiven for asking again, why bother?

The fact is, that at some point in our lives we can all lose our jobs, we can all be between jobs, and most of us in those circumstances, would turn to the benefit office to assist us in paying our rent.

If as an agent we stated right at the outset that we would only take tenants in full time employment, that's fine, but there is nothing to say that an existing employed tenant might not become redundant two month's down the line. If that happened, the chances are, you would have a tenant on your books on Housing Benefit, regardless of your up front restrictions, regardless of your initial intentions. What are you going to do then?

Being in receipt of HB is not grounds for evicting someone. Whether you like it or not, it might be better to know how the system works.

TENANTS ON BENEFIT

Here are some specific examples of tenants of mine who were in receipt of HB. In my last year as a property manager I had a former Nat West bank manager who'd recently been made redundant, an unemployed solicitor who looked over a few things of mine when he had nothing better to do, and a lecturer from Bristol

University between posts, and they were <u>all</u> on Housing Benefit.

Were they bad tenants? Of course not! They were in fact excellent tenants in every other respect. So why not entertain tenants such as these in the first place?

The fact is there are some people on Housing Benefit you might consider, and some you wouldn't, just the same as employed people. If you rejected them all out of hand because they were on benefit, you would be harming your own business, because you would be missing that business. I suggest you at least consider Housing Benefit cases, no more, no less, consider every case carefully on its merits.

What sort of tenants wouldn't I take? I had four lads aged eighteen and nineteen none of whom were working. I didn't consider housing them, would you? They might have been really nice kids, but they could go and live somewhere else as far as I was concerned. I go back the Me-Me-Me test. Would I consider placing those guys unsupervised in my own house? If the answer was no, that would be the end of it as far as I was concerned. The answer **was** no! Fait accompli.

I respect your views if you decide against any benefit cases in any circumstances, and I'm sure you will run a successful business regardless, it's just that it won't expand as rapidly as it might otherwise. And let's face it; we are in the property business to make money. We want to grow as quickly as we can. And I'll tell you another thing, some landlords LIKE housing benefit tenants. I kid you not. This applies especially in the poorer areas, and I'm using the word 'poorer' in connection with the housing stock.

In areas of poor quality housing, landlords often look upon Housing Benefit as kindly as the tenants do, they rely on it; fact is they would be in trouble without it. They don't want to see the system changed too much, or worse still, abolished, as some people would like.

So now I guess you want me to tell you precisely how the Housing Benefit Scheme works in your area, and I'd tell you, except the system varies from one local authority to another. Standardisation has yet to fully hit the HB market. Perhaps one day it will, but it isn't here yet. Nevertheless this will give you a general idea:

HOUSING BENEFIT GENERAL GUIDELINES

Housing Benefit, and from now one I'm going to refer to is as HB is assessed on a weekly basis. Each person is assessed separately, based on their individual circumstances, so even if you owned four identical houses in a row, all rented out to four tenants in receipt of HB, it is quite feasible you would receive four different payments.

Once the applicant has lodged his or her claim with the HB office, and I'll return to their claim forms in a minute or two, in some areas a low interim payment is sanctioned quite quickly. Perhaps £35 a week when in fact the property may well be assessed at £80 pw.

The claim form then drops onto an almighty pile of similar claims that are then waded through by the hard-pressed HB staff. I am convinced that the tenants and agents who enquire of the progress of these claims most often, who ring, nay pester, the HB office, are the ones whose claims are sorted the quickest. I am sure the HB office would deny this, and won't thank me for saying so, but I speak as I find. In other words if you have a lazy tenant who couldn't give a fig whether the paperwork is processed or not, you will almost certainly be kept waiting a lot longer before your payments begin to flow.

The rent officer inspects the claim and he will then assess the final payment the benefit office will make. In many cases he will need to visit the tenant in the property. He might check out the standard of the house or flat, he might have additional questions for the tenant, perhaps regarding a previous benefit claim, but they don't visit the house every time. It may be that there's been a benefit tenant in that house or a very similar property before. The rent officer may know the house and the area well. It may be that the tenant has claimed before, and in these circumstances the assessing officer may make his decision without ever moving from his desk.

When they have decided what benefit is to be paid, they will write to the tenant and advise them of the figure. They will also write to the agent, if there is one, providing the tenant has ticked a particular box on their application form authorising them so to do.

There is no definitive time that you can rely on between lodging the claim and receiving the first cash payment from the benefit office, but 5 weeks would be a fair guess, 10 weeks not unheard of. It depends on how much of a backlog there is your area, and how much of a sense of urgency your tenant possesses, not to mention how straight they are. A backlog of some proportion is the one thing you can rely on.

KEEPING LANDLORDS INFORMED
KEEPS LANDLORDS HAPPY

If there is going to be a delay in rent flowing, and there almost certainly will be if you are relying on HB, the landlord would need to be made aware that payments would not start until the assessment process had been completed.

In other words a landlord housing a tenant in receipt of benefit may have to wait up to three months before they receive any payment, unless the tenant could be persuaded to make rental payments upfront in the intervening period, always assuming they were capable, and agreeable, to doing such a thing.

When that happens the tenant would need to be reimbursed for any credit balance on their rent account once the housing benefit payments kicked in. In my experience most tenants will be hassling you for the refund the moment it is due. That is their right of course.

The payments are almost always backdated to the date of the claim, which should coincide with the start date of the tenancy agreement. Tenants should make a claim as early as possible. In fact they can claim up to 13 weeks prior to becoming entitled to benefit, so if they know they will be moving in to a particular address they can set the ball rolling straight away.

In most geographical areas, but not all, payments are made in four-weekly tranches. Thus, if a tenant were finally assessed at £75 per week the payment on the Schedule would be £300 for that tenant for a four weekly period. The dates that the payment covered are listed on the Schedule supplied by the benefit office, so you can keep an accurate track of which weeks you have been paid for.

HOW ARE BENEFIT PAYMENTS MADE?

And to whom? When the tenant fills out their application form, they need to fill in various boxes that relate to the actual payment. They can decide to have the money sent direct to themselves, either straight into their bank account, or more usually, via a giro cheque posted through the mail to the tenant's address.

In theory, the tenant should then draw the money and hand it to the landlord, or landlord's agent to pay the rent. The tenant could get into trouble if they use the money for any other purpose. But of course it doesn't stop them sometimes doing so.

If you had four screaming hungry kids and £300 in your hand, you might be tempted to spend some of it, if not all, in the local supermarket, (how many of us would do the same thing given the same circumstances?) If this happens, the rent could remain unpaid, at the very least, in part.

However, the tenant has another option, in that they can sign over their benefit to be paid directly to the landlord, or landlord's agent, and the majority nowadays do this. It gives them a fairly hassle free life. They can sit back and believe the government is paying their rental direct, either in full or in part, and they have nothing to worry about. And it is true that once payments have been set up and start flowing, they can run on uninterrupted for twelve months, or more in some cases, before the HB office will look at the situation again.

BENEFIT CONTRIBUTIONS VERSUS CONTRACTED RENTAL

Imagine a situation where a tenant has passed all his references, and paid the necessary deposit. They sign a contract at £400 per month. They are in receipt of benefit and the final assessment is notified to be £85.72 per week. (Yes the figures can be as odd as that). What happens then?

If the agent, or landlord, receives £85.72 per week in four weekly slugs, the agent would receive £342.88 every four weeks. But there are thirteen 'four weekly' periods in a year so in effect the agent would receive £342.88 x 13 = £4457.44 per annum. So it follows that on a calendar monthly basis the agent is in fact receiving from the HB the equivalent of £371.45 per month. (That's the £4,457.44 divided by 12).

Still with that? I know it seems unnecessarily complicated but you need to understand the arithmetic for one very good reason. It is clear in this case that the HB is not, covering the rental in full, so the agent would need to approach the tenant and ask for the shortfall to be made up. The shortfall figure on this let would be £28.55 per month.

MAKING UP SHORTFALL FIGURES

The best way to obtain shortfalls, once the figure is known, is to ask the tenant to make a payment by standing order mandate to keep the rent account up to date. This also ensures that the account doesn't slip into arrears in the future. If it does slip into arrears over a period of time, it is very difficult to bring matters back into line later.

Some tenants in poorer property do not even have a bank account, and clearly they would not be able to pay any shortfall by SOM. You would have to ask them to call into the office and make up the shortfall in person. The shortfall figure could be larger or smaller than the figure shown here. If you are not too busy you might consider collecting it yourself from the tenant, but I would not recommend you start doing that. You'd be setting a dangerous precedent and before long they would expect you to collect it.

Imagine if you had 25 similar tenants all making up small shortfalls, and you trying to collect them all on the doorstep. Half the time the door wouldn't be opened and you'd have to return later. Imagine the time you would waste chasing around smallish amounts of cash. You won't need me to tell you that would be terrible time management. The answer is to insist that tenants pay by standing order, or send you a cheque, or deliver cash to you in person.

Alternatively some tenants ask their parents to pay the shortfall by standing order and many do. You could even suggest that idea to tenants faced with a shortfall figure. It works, and any system that produces regular rental payments should be considered.

ESTABLISH A SYSTEM AT THE OUTSET

At the beginning of the let, find out if the tenant is intending to claim HB. You'll have a very good hint if there is no employer listed on the application form. If the answer is "Yes" you should discuss with them to whom the benefit is to be paid. Do this at the earliest opportunity. Never leave it until the tenant is in the property. Remember, before the tenant signs the agreement and takes they keys, you hold all the cards, afterwards you don't.

If the tenant is intending to apply for HB insist they complete the benefit forms and lodge them at the HB office immediately. You might even consider taking the tenant to the benefit office yourself, that way you would know for certain they had indeed been there. A colleague of mine did that, and it worked very well. You could even mention to the landlord, "Yes Mister Johnson, I know they have definitely been to the HB office because I took them there myself!"

Your landlord should be impressed by your keenness if nothing else. This is something that large agencies would never consider doing in a million years. But who cares what they do? You will run your business as you see fit, and anything that speeds up rent should be considered.

Don't forget to remind the tenant to ask the HB for a receipt for all documents lodged, as they are notorious for losing things. At a later date if they are shown a valid receipt, they will make more of an effort to trace the paperwork because they will know for a fact they have actually received the documents, as opposed to a tenant telling them porky-pies. (Yes, that does happen sometimes, unfortunately, you won't be surprised to learn).

PROS & CONS OF DIRECT PAYMENTS

There are BIG pros and cons regarding collecting benefit directly.

PROS:

1. The money comes to you and the tenant doesn't see it, and thus can't spend it
2. You can monitor clearly what is coming in and make arrangements to collect the shortfall, if any
3. You are immediately aware of any change in the scale of payments and can take action accordingly

CONS:

1. There is one huge downside of receiving benefit payments direct, and this is it. You receive rental payments from the benefit office for a particular tenant in good faith, and duly pay it over to the landlord, less your commission. If at a later date the HB office decide in their wisdom, they have overpaid you, or made a mistake in making a payment in the first place, the HB will come back to you for a partial, or in the worst case scenario, a full refund of all the monies paid to you.

Worse still they might even deduct it from a future payment Schedule without giving you the opportunity to dispute their decision. Not nice. So what can you do about that?

HB OFFICE RECLAIMING BENEFIT

Imagine if you had <u>incorrectly</u> received monies on behalf of a tenant of £95 per week for a year. You would have received £4,940 in total, and that is the figure the HB might ask you to pay back. Why might the HB office change their minds and ask for benefit back? There are several possible reasons. Perhaps the tenant lied on their application form, perhaps they were in full time employment all along, and were not entitled to housing benefit at all. Regrettably, that happens sometimes.

Your obvious next course of action would be to ask the landlord to reimburse you. Do you think you'd get it? You might, but for a start the landlord might have gone abroad. Secondly, they might not have any money. And thirdly, they might say to you, "You're the agent you should have managed it better".

If you took the landlord to court, you'd probably win, but that's messy and unproductive, and time consuming, and who wants to gain a reputation for suing their own clients?

The answer is, to vet your tenants very carefully from day one. If you have any doubts about them, any gut feeling that everything is not quite as it should be, bin the application. Never turn a blind eye to dodgy housing benefit claims, for they will surely come back to haunt you big time at a later date.

ASSESSING BENEFIT APPLICANTS

Here are some further tips that might help you in your assessing procedure:

The prospective tenant says, "Oh yeah, my fella will be living with us, but I don't want him to be on the tenancy agreement, it helps with the benefit, you know what I mean?" Wink, wink.

Answer: NO! If the chap is going to be living in the house, his name must be on the tenancy agreement. Period. Why wouldn't it be? The HB will want to see the tenancy agreement and the benefit will be assessed accordingly. In this case the bloke is quite likely to be employed. What they are proposing is illegal, and a blatant attempt to defraud the HB office. Remember HB is ultimately paid for by all of us, the taxpayers, and fraud could never be encouraged.

The prospective tenant says, "I've been working abroad so I can't give you a landlords or credit reference".

Answer: It's amazing how many people who want to claim benefit have suddenly returned from abroad. (It might be true, but just as likely it could be a fib, and they could be hiding from their appalling track record of previous poor payment.) Ask them to produce proof of earnings whilst working abroad, and ask them for an employer's reference anyway. There's nothing to stop you emailing a company in Nova Scotia, or anywhere else, for a reference. The world's a small place these days.

But it can still be difficult to credit reference someone who's been living in Wagga Wagga or Swaziland, (does Swaziland still exist?) and clued-up tenants know this. I'd be very suspicious of any application hiding behind the, "We've been working abroad" excuse unless they could produce full documentary history of their recent employment record. Demand a first class guarantor anyway. No guarantor, then bin it.

Then there's the prospective tenant who says, "You can have all the benefit, but I won't be able to make up any shortfall," as if they are doing you a favour.

Answer: The shortfall might be three quarters of the total rental! No shortfall payments, no tenancy, simple as, bin that too.

MOST REBATES ARE FULLY JUSTIFIED

In reality, the vast majority of HB payments that have to be reimbursed to the HB office are payments that have been made by them for a period clearly **after** the tenant left the property. In other words the HB office didn't put a stop on the rental payments quickly enough.

In those cases you should have known the tenant had left, and in that case you should have held on to that money and not paid the landlord for any portion of rental paid for any period AFTER the tenancy had expired. The rule is:

BENEFIT PAYMENTS RECEIVED FOR A PERIOD <u>AFTER</u> THE TENANCY ENDED ARE INCORRECT. THEY SHOULD **NOT** BE PASSED TO THE LANDLORD BUT BE HELD PENDING REFUND TO THE HB.

In effect, that rental should still be sitting in your clients' bank account, (gaining interest by the way, so all is not so terrible) and you should be able to reimburse the benefit office quickly and fully. Get into the habit of returning overpaid rental to the benefit office whenever they ask for it. If you don't, it could mount up quickly, and they are inclined to become a lot more excited about it as the numbers increase. It's not unknown for them to appoint outside debt collectors either to chase overpaid cash on their behalf, and that is the last thing you would want.

<u>WHY BOTHER?</u>

After all that, it wouldn't surprise me if you never wanted to hear the words Housing Benefit ever again, yet despite everything, there are still very good reasons not to automatically jettison the idea.

<u>MOST REFERENCED HOUSING BENEFIT TENANTS ARE GREAT – REALLY, THEY ARE!</u>

The vast majority of tenants claiming HB are great. I had one with a missing foot, a pretty genuine case there you would think, another who was so badly asthmatic, he couldn't climb the few stairs into our office, I had to meet and greet him in the street when he paid his shortfall, which he never once missed, and yet another who'd broken his back when he fell off a crane.

To put it in perspective, out of every fifty HB tenants I dealt with, I would estimate we only ever had a problem with perhaps two or three, and that's not so different to employed tenants.

Anyone, and I mean anyone, can lose their job and they would then normally be entitled to help from the government towards their housing costs. You have to be selective. Some people you take, and some you don't. It's important you don't let your selection standards slip, and always keep your wits about you.

NEVER take someone on HB that you believe is not being truthful with you, because they are probably not being truthful with the HB office either

And NEVER, EVER house a tenant, or turn a blind eye, knowing full well that an application was in any way fraudulent. You might benefit in the short term. You could end up in clink in the longer term. It is not worth it!

A quick recap:

Reference all potential HB tenants in the same manner
Thoroughly, carefully and accurately
Monitor HB payments rigorously
<u>Always</u> collect shortfalls

PRE TENANCY DETERMINATIONS

A pre tenancy determination, a PTD, is a procedure that many tenants in receipt of HB like to follow. In short, it involves the potential tenant filling out a simple one or two page form that is then signed by the landlord or the landlord's agent. You can sign a PTD in the sure and certain knowledge that you are NOT committing yourself, or your landlord, to a tenancy agreement. The potential tenant then lodges the signed PTD form at the benefit office.

The benefit office will examine the form and produce an **estimate** of the housing benefit they will pay against a particular property. The sole point of a PTD is to assist tenants to check whether they will be able to afford a particular house. The benefit office then send a copy of their estimate to both the tenant and the agent or landlord, and they usually turn PTD's around very quickly, within a day or two.

The PTD estimate is not binding, only the final application for Housing Benefit will ascertain that, but it is a useful exercise. For example, if a particular house you manage is priced at the equivalent of £100 per a week, and the PTD comes back at £90, you and the tenant would have a good idea that the tenant would need to produce only £10 a week in top-up rent to meet the rental requirement in full. You can discuss with the tenant whether they are comfortable with that, and whether they wish to proceed.

But if the PTD came back at only £40 per week, clearly the tenant would have a much greater shortfall to find, and this might make it difficult for the tenant to proceed. The greater the shortfall, the greater the care you should take before proceeding further. You must be confident the tenant has the means to make up any such shortfall. Ask them where it would be coming from?

You should be aware that some landlords are not happy with a PTD being carried out, although they are few and far between. The reason for this is that there have been some cases where a landlord may have had a house on at say £100 per week, and a PTD was done and came back, after looking at that particular applicant's individual circumstances at a low figure, of say £35 per week.

There is some evidence to suggest that should that tenant decide not to proceed, and subsequently you located a second tenant and they then requested a PTD, the HB may simply look at their file and say "that house has already been assessed and the figure is £35", in other words at a much lower figure than it would have been if the PTD had not been carried out in the first place.

In my experience, very few landlords object to PTD's, and for the most part they serve a useful purpose both for the tenant and the agent. If in doubt, clear it with the landlord first.

YOU NEED TO DO YOUR HOMEWORK

I hope I haven't put you off benefit cases altogether because that is not my intention. What I have tried to do is make you more aware of some of the hazards and difficulties that you could come across in your future dealings.

If you decide to consider benefit cases, make the effort to go and visit the benefit office, collect all the bumf they have to offer (and believe me, they have bumf in spades!) Try and make a personal contact there, someone you can talk to for advice and assistance, and then set up a Payment Schedule. This is the vehicle that will transfer funds directly into your clients' account.

The HB will require from you proof of identification among other things, as well as assurance that you are NOT related to the tenants. If the tenant was your niece or aunty, the chances are that you would be barred from collecting the HB. This is because they are very concerned about fraud, and rightly so, and may conclude that you have a conflict of interest, representing a landlord on the one hand, and a tenant, a member of your own family, on another.

Once you have set up a Schedule, payments will automatically appear in your bank account and will be supported by a hard copy arriving in the post, (once a tenant has successfully completed the necessary paperwork).

Read all the information you can find, and become an expert in completing benefit application forms. Then you can advise others. If the rules say two forms of ID are necessary, there is no point in going to the office with only one, or worse still, none. Everything will come to a complete standstill. How does that ad go, "It does what it says on the tin!" Housing Benefit forms are the same, if they say they need to see the tenancy agreement; they need to see the tenancy agreement! Don't let the tenant turn up without it. It will only delay things, and you, and they, will have to return again on another day. More time lost, more time wasted.

Learn, teach yourself, and study, and you will quickly become the biggest expert on HB in your area. You will quickly get to grips with it, and before long you will notice landlords asking you for advice on how the system works, and what they should do next.

Charge them £50 an hour for your advice, I'm serious, you could save a landlord hundreds of pounds with one simple piece of expertise, once you have become that expert. Place it as an additional service in your Fact Pack. "Housing Benefit Consultations: £50".

And one final word: I must emphasise that everything in this chapter is subject to change. HB offices throughout the country may differ, procedures differ too; you know what local bureaucracy is like. They can't leave anything alone for too long. It is for you to keep abreast of changes in your area, no one else can do that for you. So please don't write to me and say, "You said such and such and it's baloney!" I'm telling you exactly as I've found it, but that does not mean you will find it the same where you live. Here are a few more tips and facts about HB that you might find useful.

- It is sometimes referred to as rent rebate or rent allowance
- Tenants do not have to be in receipt of other benefit to qualify

- If the tenant has savings over £3,000, this could affect the amount they receive
- There are special rules applying to anyone under 25
- Tenants cannot claim benefit if they are living in a close relative's household
- Most full time students do not qualify for benefit
- The maximum housing benefit payable is the rental stated on the tenancy agreement
- Tenants who receive a low figure and are convinced it is wrong, can ask the local authority to look at the claim again
- If a tenant goes into a nursing home they will usually lose their entitlement to HB

You can access a deep mine of additional information on the subject of Housing Benefit at this website:
www.dwp.gov.uk/lifeevent/benefits/housing_benefit.asp

ARE YOU UP FOR THE CHALLENGE?

Aim to become **The** expert
on all matters housing benefit.
There is a shortage of such people.
Who knows?
You might even derive
some strange satisfaction in doing so.

Fifteen:
Your Business Progresses

You've launched your business, your advertising campaign is well under way, and you have let your first properties, trousering your first fees. You've learnt a great deal about your local housing benefit systems, and that might be something you never expected to know. But how is your business progressing, and what can you do to push it along?

There will be days when nothing seems to happen, the phone doesn't ring, a landlord you may have had great hopes for has chosen another. They can be fussy devils, and you have to expect that sometimes. You might start to become a little disillusioned, depressed even, and when that happens, you must recognise the signs and SNAP OUT OF IT! STOP FEELING SORRY FOR YOURSELF. MAKE THINGS HAPPEN! It is your business, and you must drive it. No one else will.

You can take comfort from the fact that every businessperson feels that way sometimes. There are some days when it's more difficult to motivate oneself than others. Your mind starts to drift away to how nice it would be to lie on the beach in Barcelona. (Is there a beach in Barcelona? I don't know).

But it is precisely on days like these when nothing much seems to happen, that you should be aggressively promoting your business, for the simple reason that you have the time to do so.

PROMOTE YOUR BUSINESS FEROCIOUSLY

Take a look at every tenant's application form you have ever received, whether you have rejected the tenant or not. You will find one and possibly two landlord's names and addresses on each one. Dig the forms out and take another look. Landlord's right? Remember when you first started and you were wondering how you could contact real landlords, people with property; and there they are, staring you in the face. Turn on the computer and write them a letter, do it today.

Dear Landlord, except you might write:

Dear Mister Ramsbottom,

I am writing a brief note today to advise you that we have several excellent fully employed tenants on our books seeking property in this area right now.

(If you have been advertising in the papers during the previous four weeks you will most certainly have a supply of excellent potential tenants. Did you note their names and telephone numbers as you should have done?)

Do you have any property currently available to let? If so, we would like to offer you a 20% *(the incentive figure can be anything you like, it's your business you are in total control*) deduction on our normal fees. Please ring me at any time on my private number 07000 00000 to discuss the matter. I look forward to hearing from you soon.

Yours sincerely
Jack Boeing
Jets Lets.

Get the letters in the post quickly, not in a few days' time but today! If you post ten letters to ten landlords, I'll wager you get a call back, at least one. Remember: every signed up landlord should produce at least a 1,000.00 per year in revenue for you.

It will be worth your while pursuing them. It's a good idea to include an insurance brochure too. Even if the landlord has no property to let, they might need some additional insurance, and if they ring you and not Farquar's Lettings up the road, it is a positive sign they are thinking about you. Your aim is to encourage your local landlords to ring you about all their property matters, and if you contact them on a regular basis, sooner or later, they will.

When times are quiet it is up to you to MAKE THINGS HAPPEN, no one else will. It's your business, and it is YOU who must kick up the dust. Be imaginative; study other agent's promotional schemes. Come up with something different, something BETTER, but whatever you do, keep yourself busy promoting your agency, because your agency will become the best in the town. You know that, I know that, it's your task to demonstrate the fact to others.

YOU WILL BECOME
THE BEST AGENCY IN THE TOWN
NOTHING WILL STOP YOU!
BELIEVE IT
<u>IT WILL HAPPEN</u>

<u>TRY SIGNS</u>

Another excellent way of promoting and advertising your business is to have signs professionally made up. You know the things I mean, like the estate agent sticks up outside houses all over the area.

But I wouldn't recommend having them erected outside the property for two reasons. Firstly it's usual to pay an outside contractor to erect these signs and right from the beginning we have concentrated on ways to cut out unnecessary overheads. It's not cheap, and it's a cost you can do without.

Secondly, signs left outside can and do go missing, especially around November 5th. Instead, keep a supply in the boot of your car, and whenever you are instructed to let a property, place a sign in the front window of the house, facing the road. Make sure the telephone number can be clearly seen from the street. For good orders sake it's a good idea to confirm with the owner that it is all right so to do. Once you have paid the initial costs of the signs this is a fantastic way to promote your business and it costs you absolutely nothing.

It will give you a real buzz to suddenly see your signs appearing in windows all over the town. I have let hundreds of properties using signs like these, and you can too. They can be just as effective as newspaper advertising and are much more cost efficient. Keeping them indoors means they are not going to get vandalised or go missing, and they can be used again and again and again. Just remember once you've let the property, to pick them up and take them with you for next time.

Take care where you buy them too, I have seen some ridiculous prices being quoted for the normal sized estate agency signs, and it is the usual size you want. Over £50 each I was quoted by one firm, each!

When I last bought signs I bought a hundred for £250, admittedly it was a little while ago, but they were the best buy I ever made. They work; they let houses, and are so much cheaper than newspaper advertising. In addition, the more signs you put up, the more chance you have of landlords noticing them and thinking, "My, this is an expanding go-ahead company, perhaps I should give them a try!"

You'll find a brief list of letting and estate agent sign makers at the end of this publication, or alternatively run a quick Internet search on google.

YOUR OWN PROPERTY PORTFOLIO

And what about your own property register? Never forget the importance of creating your own portfolio. If you haven't started yet, due to lack of finance, the objective must be to put money aside regularly to accumulate that first deposit.

I can't tell you how excited I was when I started refurbishing my first buy-to-let. I think it must have been just before those property makeover shows started that now cram the TV schedules. Have you noticed they all say the same things? Keep the walls and carpets neutral, creams and whites, beige and light. Crikey it's so neutral I'm practically falling asleep.

Well I didn't do my house in creams and white and beige and light. I worked like a Trojan, every weekend and most evenings too. It was an old house, but big with high ceilings and that means hard work, I can tell you. When I'd finished papering and painting I bought the carpets. A lush rich maroon for the hall, landing and stairs contrasting with the Victorian style green patterned wallpaper. In the front room I laid a royal blue carpet to contrast with the yellow walls. I stood back, hands on hips and admired my handiwork. I thought it looked the bees.

The house appeared in my ad the following week and six people immediately showed interest. I couldn't wait to take the first potential tenant round. A neat attractive young woman arrived carrying a bonny baby girl and bounced into the hall smiling. She looked down the hall and up the stairs, without comment, and hurried into the living room. She looked around again and laughed noisily through her sealed lips.

"What do you think?" I asked excitedly.

"The house is great, but not the colours!" She laughed again. "Who chose them? He must have been a loony!"

Yes, well, I didn't dare mention that I'd chosen the colours, I didn't see the point. She then said she couldn't possibly live there, as she'd have to redo everything. But I let the house soon after that, and it has been full ever since. I never go there now. I've heard from the gas safety man that the tenant has redecorated the house from top to bottom, in off white, and beige, really nice it is, so the gasman says. Perhaps the less extreme makeover shows do have a point after all. Keep it neutral.

Then my dad died and left me his house. I was going to sell it, but almost at the last minute had second thoughts. Instead I set about refurbishing that one too, ready for the rental market. No bright colours this time, creams and beige in abundance.

It took me a month and I did everything myself and by the time I'd finished I was spent, I can tell you, in more ways than one, not to mention a ricked shoulder that took months to heal. My first viewer appeared the very next day, an older refined lady. I showed her round and she never said a word, never a hint of how she felt about it. I showed her into the bathroom and she took a step backwards and looked at me disdainfully.

"What?" I said.
"I hope you're going to do something about that!"
"What?" I repeated.
"The bath of course! You ARE going to replace **that**, aren't you? Surely you don't expect me to get into that!

No-one in their right mind would get into a bath like that!"

The bath was a large roll-top standalone tub, the kind of thing that has come right back into fashion in recent times, you see them in every DIY superstore nowadays. At one end of the bath were two huge old silver taps that looked like Queen Victoria herself might have used. I thought they had character.

I looked back at the bath and then at her and I didn't have the courage to tell her I had wallowed happily in that very bath for a full hour after I'd finished painting the kitchen barely two days before. She stormed out and left me standing there. I didn't change the bath, and the house let shortly afterwards. Houses do let, you see. As my good friend Michael is fond of saying, "There is a bum for every seat".

PROPERTIES DO LET

Providing a property is in reasonable condition in a safe area, it <u>will</u> let. Trust me. Remember, everyone has different tastes with regard to colours and decorating, it would be a dull world if we all liked the same thing.

Start thinking about your own properties again, property that you are going to let out when you can afford them. Visit the DIY warehouses. Check out the bathrooms and the kitchens. Become an expert. Make plans, and remember that kitchens and bathrooms do not have to cost an absolute fortune. Don't ever buy the cheapest, but buying the very dearest is a mistake too, unless you are aiming at the very top liner rentals.

If you are not going to recoup the money you spend on the property through improved rental figures, why spend it at all?

Think about accruing deposits
Think about acquiring property
THINK OUTSIDE THE BOX
THINK OFTEN
THINK BIG
THINK

Sixteen:
Computer Software & The Internet

Twenty years ago almost no one had the Internet in their home. Now practically everyone does. Twenty-five years ago almost no one had a PC; I know that for certain because I started selling them.

"A PC, what's a PC? Haven't you got any Amiga's or Atari's?"
That was a typical riposte to my urging my customers to buy a PC.
"PC's are the coming thing", I said, but not many people believed me, not back then.

Now almost everyone has a PC at home. So what are they using all this sophisticated and powerful equipment for?

To look for property of course! Property websites are now the second most frequently accessed sites on the entire web. (I'll give you one guess what the foremost is, but we won't go there!) Think property please. Every estate agent has a website; many agents have more than one. Most letting agents run their own website too and if you aspire to becoming a successful letting agent you must have a decent web presence.

Why? Because they offer unlimited worldwide advertising with as many colour pictures as you like that can be accessed anywhere on earth at very low cost, comparatively speaking.

Compare for a moment the cost of a small display ad in the local paper. Perhaps 130.00 and in a few days time it has gone forever. Your website is on, all the time, 24 hours a day, 365 days a year.

You MUST have access to the web, clued up landlords expect it, and many tenants now use it to locate suitable rental property.

It only remains for you to decide which type of site to go for. Broadly speaking you have four choices:

1. Your own bespoke site. Individually designed to your requirements incorporating precisely the features you want

2. An off the shelf site you could adapt to your own use

3. Rent space on other larger property sites

4. Create your own site

YOUR OWN BESPOKE SITE

If you have the money, you might like to look at the first option. But it will cost you a fair amount of cash, I saw one firm quoting 1,000.00 in today's daily paper, and one small word of warning. Make certain when the site name is registered YOU OWN the site outright. A friend of mine had an antiques site and after a while he became dissatisfied with his site hosting company. So he gave notice to terminate the contract and move to another host.

A few days later he received an email from his service provider politely telling him that he could certainly move, but the site name would be staying with the host because they had registered it and still owned the website name. Despite the fact my friend had spent thousands of pounds promoting the name, and owned the actual physical business shipping antiques worldwide, he discovered he didn't own his own blessed website.

Cheekily the host offered to sell it to him, for a thousand pounds. He declined. When you start your own website, make absolutely certain it is YOU who owns the name. There is nothing worse than spending time and money building up a successful site, only to discover that you don't in fact have any ongoing rights to it.

Before you buy, shop around and then haggle like crazy, for there is a huge range of companies offering sites at greatly differing prices. Check out some of the sites they have previously prepared and ask yourself this, are they really good enough? There has been a huge leap forward in the quality of sites in the past few years and there is no excuse now for any site to look cheap, nasty, and homemade, especially if it isn't. Video, sound, video tours are all becoming the norm, and they are also becoming cheaper to produce, and easier for the virtual novices to do themselves.

ADAPTING AN EXISTING PACKAGE

Option 2 is something I used for a while. There are numerous companies who offer off-the-shelf property website packages though they do frequently come and go. Again, google: PROPERTY LETTING WEBSITE SOFTWARE or something similar and you will receive thousands of potential contacts. Just make sure the companies offering these services are well established and their products are easy to update for your own use.

Perhaps you may come across a landlord who doesn't want to use an agent for most of their business but would not be averse to advertising their properties on the Internet. You could take outside advertising, for a fee, and you could fix your site advertising fees as high or as low as you wish, but it's always a good idea to set them competitively to begin with, to attract a quantity of properties on to the site.

Don't forget, the more properties and information on your pages, the more interesting it will be to viewers.

The longer a browser is gazing at your web pages, the more likely they are to purchase one of your services. The trick to keep them connected is to make sure there is loads of content; and interesting content at that.

Be bold, and invite five or six other smaller independent agencies both in your area and further afield. (There will soon be lots of smaller agents than you.) Some of these agents may not have a website of their own and if you can offer them the facility of putting ALL their properties (an unlimited number) on your site including colour photographs for a small fixed fee, they might jump at the chance.

Perhaps you could charge them 30.00 per month, payable by standing order into your account, to allow them to put their properties on your site, regardless of quantity. They would actually do all the uploading too, it's simple to do, and you would not have to do a thing, other than check their money was in your bank account every month. If you signed up ten agents at 30.00 per month, that would produce over a year, a more than useful 3,600.00, yet another possible way for you to contribute toward your property deposits.

If you were going to offer this service to other agents it would be a good idea not to call your website by the name you were trading as. For example if you were trading as BRENT'S RENTS other agents might be unlikely to feel comfortable placing their houses on a site of the same name.

But if you chose a more general title, such as SMARTPROPERTY or PROPERTYEXPRESS or SOUTHCOASTHOMES or HUNTAHOME (subject to the names being available), other independent agencies would be more likely to use your site. Again, you could charge whatever you liked. Your initial aim would be to get as much interesting content on to the site, and as quickly as possible, which in turn would attract the required traffic, which in turn again, would attract more users. It's that snowball effect again.

RENTING SPACE ON OTHER PROPERTY SITES

The third alternative web presence is to rent space on an existing site and I suspect initially this may be the best option for you. There are countless numbers of sites now available ranging from the very famous rightmove.co.uk and fish4homes.co.uk down to specialist rental only sites.

No doubt the bigger sites will be quite expensive if you can get on them, but they do have thousands and thousands of hits every day. That's what you want of course, lots of hits, readers, call it what you will.

You might like to check some of these out to see exactly what they have to offer. Most of them will accept your properties to let, for a fee of course.

www.assertahome.com
www.assuredpropertyrentals.co.uk
www.cdproperty.co.uk
www.dauntons.co.uk
www.davisestates.co.uk
www.excel-property.co.uk
www.fish4homes.co.uk
www.foxtons.co.uk
www.halfapercent.com
www.home.co.uk
www.home-sale.co.uk
www.hotproperty.co.uk
www.housesearch.co.uk
www.lettingweb.co.uk
www.lookproperty.co.uk
www.net-lettings.co.uk
www.paramountproperties.co.uk
www.pebblebeachmedia.co.uk

nothing. It will keep your clients on your site, it will keep them coming back, and it will get people talking about you.

You'll find details of affiliate marketing companies in the trade directory at the back of this book, and you should receive full details of these services from the affiliate and hosting companies if and when you decide to sign up with them.

Lastly, you might also consider running Google Ads on your site. You see them everywhere; those boxes of various sizes filled with little teaser ads and a moniker that says something like: Ads from Google.

Google really will pay you every time someone clicks through to their ads placed on your site. It is a super way of adding an extra revenue stream on your property websites. They will also automatically feature ads from property themed companies, but don't worry about inviting your direct competitors onto your site if you don't want you. You can specifically bar ads from any business that you do not want to see featured. I find that Google ads actually enhance sites, rather than detract from them, and if it brings in sufficient revenue to pay for the cost of the sites, then that must be a good thing. Google: Google Advertising, if you want more information on that, if you do not already have an account with them.

UPDATE YOUR WEBSITE

Make sure you update your site regularly, daily if you possibly can. There is nothing worse than viewing a site when it says something like, "Site last updated August 16th", when it's February. I actually saw a site the other day that proudly said: "last updated July 15th 2002. As I write, it is summer 2008!

And when your site is finished and ready, remember the most important thing to do is to promote it. There is no point in having a brilliant site that no one knows about. Put your web address on absolutely everything, your letterheads, your business cards and compliment slips, your shop window ads, your fact pack, your signs, on the back of your car, even at the foot of your emails, but don't spam! (Spam is sending out uninvited cold calling emails. That is now illegal in Great Britain.)

But you could put an additional message at the foot of all your daily outgoing emails:

"Lots of Super Property to let right now on www.prowseshouses.co.uk"

or something similar.

But the most important place to publicise your website address is within your weekly newspaper advertising in as large size letters as space permits.

It is from here that you will generate the vast majority of your hits. People use the web more and more with each passing month, especially for anything to do with property matters. I read the other day that 78,000 new users are joining the web worldwide EVERY DAY. People **will** look at your site. When they do, you must hook 'em!

PROPERTY MANAGEMENT SOFTWARE

Selecting which computer software you are going to use is an important decision and shouldn't be rushed. Check out everything that is available because it can be very difficult, time consuming, and expensive, to switch horses at a later date.

For accounting software for small and medium sized business, Sage is now the undisputed market leader. All accountants know how it works inside out and it will speed up your annual audit, but before you dash out and buy Sage, consider purchasing or leasing a full property package, because many of these now include accounting software. Quickbooks too is another package that many small businesses use, though I confess I did not find it so easy to set up.

Probably the most famous and widely used lettings package today is called CARL. Computer Aided Residential Lettings, though there are many other comparable packages available. CARL is based in Shaw, near Oldham up on the edge of the Pennines. They now have hundreds of users throughout the UK and because they have such a broad user base, they have been able to introduce many sophisticated improvements into the system in recent years.

I believe they are still operating on the basis that you cannot buy the system outright but choose to rent or lease it on a monthly basis. You will find their website listed in the trade directory at the end of this book. They offer training, both on site and in house, and any number of seminars that are very useful. They offer software that produces contracts, dozens of different standard letters, sections on housing benefit, fact packs, and so much more paperwork, some of which you undoubtedly will never use.

I don't know the current state of their website services but it would not surprise me if they were now all-encompassing. Whether you go with them or not, please do take a look at the product, and what they have to offer. It will broaden your mind and your knowledge immensely as to what is available. Ask for a FREE sample disk and you will see for yourself what it can do. It's not perfect, computer programs rarely are, but it has a tremendous amount to offer. Go here: www.carlcomms.co.uk

Other property software products you might consider are Rentacomm, Key data, and Professional Property Letting. I know absolutely nothing of these products; you will find their web names in the trade directory at the end of this book. Check them out thoroughly, and if you are considering signing up with them, ask them to supply you with the addresses of some satisfied users. As they say on the stock market bulletin boards, DYOR, Do Your Own Research. If they can't or won't supply you with satisfied customers to check out, use someone else.

But if you are ultra cost conscious, how about this? Take a look at EZPZ. They do a start-up light landlord software package from as little as 19.95. You can check out everything they have to offer at www.ezpzsoftware.co.uk

Seventeen:
Gas & Electrical Safety Checks

As an agent or property owner, you have a direct responsibility to ensure that there is a Gas Safety Certificate on your file <u>BEFORE</u> you place a tenant into a property.

NEVER place a tenant into a property where there is gas, unless you have a gas safety certificate on your file, or have had sight of a valid certificate, and in that case, obtain a photocopy for your records.

<u>THE HISTORY OF CORGI</u>

Gas Safety Inspections MUST be carried out ANNUALLY and MUST be carried out by a suitably qualified CORGI registered engineer. Corgi stands for the Confederation for the Registration of Gas Installers. It came into being in 1970 following the disaster at Ronan Point, a 22 storey block of flats in east London that was devastated by a massive gas blast in 1968.

That disaster claimed five lives and led to a determination to protect the general public from unsafe gas appliances. Today, there are approximately 48,000 registered companies belonging to CORGI employing just under 100,000 operatives. Only a CORGI registered plumber may issue a gas safety certificate. Check on the issued document for the CORGI logo. One copy of the certificate should be left in the property with the tenant, and another retained on file in the Agent's office.

If a landlord refuses to produce a certificate you must either arrange for one to be completed yourself, and deduct the cost of it from the landlord's account, stating that it is a legal requirement so to do, or alternatively, DON'T LET THE PROPERTY.

There is no room for manoeuvre on this issue. If the authorities ever carried out a spot check, as they sometimes do, and you failed to produce a valid certificate, or God forbid there was ever a serious incident in one of the properties that you managed, you and the landlord would be in serious trouble.

SEVERE PENALTIES FOR NON-COMPLIANCE

It is not unknown for a prison sentence to be imposed on parties who do not adhere to this vitally important procedure. Unbelievably, some greedy landlords still try and get away with not incurring this expense. If you let the property, you MUST ensure a valid Gas Safety Certificate is in place. It is also essential that you diarise the certificate's expiry date in order that you can arrange a fresh one be carried out next year. Like car tax disks, they are only valid for 12 months.

Only last week (Summer 2008) there was case widely publicised in the newspapers of a landlord who failed to have the gas appliances checked and the tenant's daughter was subsequently killed in her sleep through carbon monoxide poising.

If you don't adhere to this legislation how would you like to explain to distressed parents that their young son or daughter had been gassed to death in one of the properties that you managed, because you couldn't be bothered to spend 50.00 or so to have the gas appliances checked? Exactly, you wouldn't. For me, this is the single most important point on any property you intend to let.

Find a Corgi Registered Plumber. Get a Certificate BEFORE you move anyone into the house. It's simple; make sure it is done, EVERY YEAR. And don't forget to charge the landlord for all costs incurred.

ELECTRICAL SAFETY

In the United Kingdom electrical safety in any property is not quite so clear-cut, in that you are not responsible for having an annual check and certificate on file. However both the agent, and the landlord have a duty of care towards the tenant to ensure the electrics are checked and safe.

On all let property you must ensure that the electrical system and all appliances supplied by you are safe - failure to comply with the regulations is a criminal offence and could result in:

- A fine of £5,000 per item for not complying
- Six month's imprisonment

- Possible manslaughter charges in the event of deaths
- The tenant may also sue the agent and the landlord for civil damages
- Your property insurance could also be invalidated.
- The Health & Safety Executive enforces the regulations.
- There is no statutory requirement to have annual safety checks on electrical equipment as there is with gas, but it is advisable for landlords to have periodic checks carried out by a qualified electrician

I strongly suggest you discuss the matter with your landlord and if there is any doubt, especially if you notice worn cabling, loose plugs and sockets, and dated equipment, you should insist those matters are addressed immediately. Don't take any risks; in the longer run your landlords will thank you for keeping them straight and legal.

It is also important that you ensure that ALL electrical appliances supplied by you or the landlord are safe and in good working order. One way to avoid this problem is **not** to supply electrical appliances, or as few as you need to. Most tenants have their own things anyway, and you are not responsible for their equipment. Keep receipts of new appliances that are introduced, and replace and discard any old ones.

Periodic inspections by a qualified electrician are a very good idea. Keep records of these inspections too. Act on any recommendations. Think twice about managing properties where the electrics are obviously out of date and the landlord won't do anything to update them.

THINK SAFETY FIRST – ALWAYS

This is **NOT** an area where monetary savings can ever be made. Would you put up with dodgy electrics in your own home? Of course you wouldn't! Neither should anyone else have to.

FURNITURE FIRE SAFETY

There is one other aspect of SAFETY you need to bear in mind and that is FIRE SAFETY, particularly to do with fire retardant furniture.

Where a property is furnished, the landlord may only supply soft furnishings where they comply with the latest fire safety regulations. This particularly relates to foam filled furniture that must bear the fire retardant kite mark. If it does not, this furniture must not be supplied to the tenant.

You, as the agent, have a responsibility to check that there is no illegal furniture within the premises and if you find any that is, it is your duty to advise the landlord to have it removed forthwith. This especially applies to settees, sofas, chairs and beds.

Most landlords are fully aware of their responsibilities when it comes to providing modern fire resistant furniture. The easiest thing to do to comply with this legislation is to have any old foam filled furniture removed and taken to the local tip. Charity shops will not touch them either for precisely the same reason. This is one of the main reasons why so many landlords prefer to let unfurnished property. If there is no furniture in the house, you can't break any fire safety rules.

Double-check it. Does the property include any soft furniture that does not bear the kitemarks? If it does, advise the landlord to remove or replace it. If they won't, and the let goes ahead anyway, both YOU and the LANDLORD could be held accountable if there was a fire at any time during the tenancy. Why take the risk? And, <u>never</u> put old foam filled furniture into any property you may own, even if the tenant has no money and no furniture at all, you must not supply such items.

You would be far better off to let the property unfurnished, even if the rental figure was slightly less. You are talking life and death here, it is as important as that. Penalties are rightly harsh for transgressors. Make sure you understand your responsibilities.

<u>KEEP LEGAL, KEEP SAFE.</u>

Finally, there is a relatively new requirement that instruction manuals and booklets are left in the property for ALL gas and electrical appliances. It's a good idea to establish a file containing these booklets in the kitchen drawer. It is a good idea to keep photocopies too, because they are always going missing. You can point these booklets out to tenants when they move in. Make sure they are still there when the tenant moves out again.

<u>SAFETY IS PARAMOUNT</u>
<u>IT GOES WITHOUT SAYING</u>

Eighteen:
Additional Revenue Streams

To date we have looked at nine potential income streams, namely:

1. Tenants processing Fees
2. Landlords one off fee on managed properties
3. Landlords monthly management percentage fee
4. Landlords one off fee on unmanaged properties
5. Inventory Fees
6. Housing Benefit Consultation Fees
7. Interest gained on positive cash flow
8. Selling advertising on your website
9. Commission gained through click thru's on your website

But it doesn't end there. All good and successful agencies make sure they boost their earnings from additional revenue streams and it makes sense that you do too.

Here are another four excellent potential income streams that you can establish and build up very quickly for little outlay. Don't worry if some credits are only small to begin with, it's all grist to the mill, and as your business grows, so will many of these streams. Confucius he say, "Many streams make a flood". Well I don't suppose he did, but you get the drift.

INSURANCE

You really should be selling insurance policies from day one. Why? Because they entail very little work, and policies can run on for years and years. Many landlords opt to pay their property insurance premiums by monthly direct debit through their letting agents and every time they do so, you get a payment.

Every year they renew, you get a payment. Typical commission is 20% of the total premiums. That may not sound a lot by itself, but look at this:

With the huge increase in house prices over the past ten years, and the big increase in insurance premiums too, a typical let semi detached house now costs around 500.00 per year to insure. If you have a hundred properties on your book, and if you work at it, you will reach that figure sooner than you might think, and if you insured them all, that's 20% of 50,000, that's 10,000 a year, EVERY YEAR!

That ten thousand would be paid straight into your bank account. That ten thousand could be the deposit on your very first property to let, and the beauty is you wouldn't have done a lot of work to earn it. Sell insurance, it is easy, it pays well and it makes sense.

The commission you earn is transferred directly into your bank account, or in some cases you deduct it at source when selling the policy. You get paid for filling out one form. In the second year you get paid for doing absolutely nothing. Every year that policy is renewed, you get paid, and some policies will run on for ten, fifteen, even twenty years.

As well as landlords' buildings insurance, there are numerous other policies available, such as tenants' contents, landlords' legal expenses, and many others as well.

I always made a point of writing to every new tenant after they had moved into one of our properties, welcoming them with an up beat happy kind of letter, and I enclosed a tenants' contents insurance policy brochure. Some tenants have no idea that they are responsible for insuring their own possessions when they rent a house.

One agent I know actually sends his tenants one of those greetings card type things, "Hope you are Happy in you New Home". He tucks an insurance brochure inside as well. The tenant might send off the application form direct to the insurer together with their cheque and you probably won't even know about it, until a payment shows up in your bank account from your grateful insurance broker. Do it, it works, it really does.

Incidentally, with regard to contents, especially in furnished or part furnished properties, the landlord is responsible for insuring <u>their</u> contents; the tenant is responsible for insuring <u>theirs</u>. So if you see a tenant moving in a giant sized flatscreen television set, do them a favour and advise them to make sure they get insured.

"Oh and by the way, here's a brochure, why don't you fill it in and send it off, pay it monthly if you prefer, it's only a few pounds".

They do it, and you get paid. You'll also be in line for a big thank you, from them, if they ever get burgled.

Keep a supply of insurance brochures in the car: you never know when you might need one, you never know when an opportunity might arise to hand them out. They are FREE when you sign up with one of the big agencies.

BUY-TO-LET MORTGAGES

Oh no! I hear you cry, I don't want to get involved in mortgages under any circumstances! The good news is, you don't have to. All you need do is hand out buy-to-let mortgage brochures to new and existing landlords, and to anyone else, such as friends and family, who you think might be interested in buying property for letting or living purposes.

Everything is then arranged directly between the mortgage provider and the person taking out the mortgage. Your only involvement is to distribute brochures bearing your ID number or stamp and admire the commission that dumps into your bank account. This commission can easily top a thousand pounds on a single mortgage. Worth handing out a brochure for, don't you think? Where can you obtain the brochures? Try Homelet or Letsure.

UTILITY SUPPLIES

Telephones, gas, electricity and Internet. You can reduce your landlords and your own costs on all of these. How? By taking out an agency with one of the utility companies operating in these fields. Telecom Plus is one company that offer these services through their Utility Warehouse brand, but there are many others and it is worth looking into.

The clients who sign on usually do not need to change their supply equipment. There is no interruption to service, sometimes no contract to sign, meaning that the user can return to their traditional supplier at any time if they really want to, and with some of the service suppliers, there are no numbers or codes to dial on land line telephone calls.

You could easily incorporate an agency into your business and earn commissions on all the customers you introduce. You are in an excellent position to do so. You can save your clients money on all their gas, electricity and telephones in all of their properties. You could send a brochure to your tenants too, along with the one for insurance. Everyone wants extra money in their pockets don't they? especially with the hard hitting credit crunch. This is one way of doing precisely that.

And when you finally start to build your own portfolio, make sure your own houses are switched to the utility supplier that can offer you lower costs and additional commission.

PROPERTY REPAIRS

Every property you own or manage will require repairs sooner or later, even the new ones, and you need to establish your own system to deal with them. Imagine an irritated tenant who rings you first thing in the morning and complains that they have been without electricity since 8pm the previous night. What do you do?

Check the file to ascertain if there are instructions there as to who will sort out maintenance problems. If you manage the property for a landlord you should have discussed with them at the outset who would deal with maintenance matters. If you are instructed to sort the problem, consider whether there is a trip switch in the property. It could be something very simple, such as a blown light bulb that may have set off the trip switch, turning off all the electricity.

You'll usually find the switch in the main electricity cupboard. It happens quite often in my house, usually on a cold dark January night when a bulb pops. My electric cupboard happens to be outside on the side of the building, and not just the meter boxes, but the fuses as well. My electrician tells me that modern day systems are deliberately designed that way as a safety feature, to trip the electric, hair trigger - they're meant to do it. But that is little comfort when they go off on a cold wet night

If there is a trip switch, you may already know where it is. Simply ask the tenant to flip it back and the problem is often solved. If there isn't a switch, or turning the switch hasn't solved the problem, you obviously need the services of a qualified electrician.

It is always a good idea to discuss with any landlord prior to letting a property the procedures for dealing with repairs. Many landlords, especially the larger ones have their own maintenance person, or even a team of trade people standing by for just such an emergency. In that case all you need do is ring the landlord and report the problem, and they should deal with it. If the tenant is without electricity you should emphasise the urgency of the matter. If you don't, the repair guy might take his time arriving, and in that case, you will certainly be on the end of increasingly heated telephone calls.

Where the landlord does not have any arrangement in place to deal with maintenance matters, they might ask you to deal with it. That is a very good reason to build up your own network of contacts of electricians, plumbers, decorators, joiners, glazers, gardeners, and sundry work people. Keep their numbers handy, and when you find one who is prompt, reliable and inexpensive, look after them, for they are like gold dust.

When their bill comes in, make sure you deduct it from the landlord's statement and pay the contractor as soon as you are able to do so. Build up goodwill, for there will come a time when you need help to sort out a problem at short notice. Contractors who haven't been promptly paid are unlikely to be sympathetic.

YOUR OWN MAINTENANCE DIVISION

You will find the quantity of maintenance jobs you deal with steadily increases and sooner or later the thought will occur to you that you should be carrying out the work yourself, instead of farming it out. If you did that you would have more control over the situation if you delegated one of your own staff to sort matters. BRENTS RENTS for example might set up another division, say BRENTS PROPERTY MAINTENANCE, to deal with the work that pours in. As you become more confident in overseeing maintenance contracts, you could take on additional work from outside customers too. Do you smell revenue? You should.

Of course you will need suitably qualified staff to carry out the work, perhaps a brother or relative, and you might even employ some of the same guys you used on a sub contracting basis before. If you do that, you should negotiate a trade discount, so you can pass on more or less the same charges to the landlord as before.

TAKING A MARGIN

I don't have a problem with an agent taking a margin on maintenance work, providing it is reasonable. If you are spending a great deal of time organising and solving landlords' repair problems you are, in my view, entitled to be paid for your time and expertise. You are a professional person, and if there is a small percentage mark up to cover your time, that must be fair and reasonable.

However, it has to be said that some agents abuse their position when it comes to repairs, and eventually this abuse has a habit of coming to the landlord's attention, and before you know it you have a very dissatisfied client.

One agent I knew charged his landlord 700.00 for having the outside of his house painted, that was the window frames, gables and soffits, not the rendering. I know for a fact that he beat a desperate local painter down to just 200.00 to have the work done. If you are completing work for third parties you are free to quote any price you like, and make as much margin as you can, and good luck to you. But if you are carrying out work for your own landlords, whilst at the same time taking a huge margin for yourself, there could be a conflict of interest there.

Remember, you do have a duty of care toward your landlord, they are employing you to look after their property interests, and clearly that does not include ripping him or her off with huge margins, as in that painting job.

The acid test is to ask yourself whether you would be comfortable for all the facts on any repair to be laid on the table in front of the property owner. If you were not, perhaps you should be questioning how much mark-up you were incorporating for yourself. Was it justified to cover the time element spent? You will know the answer, better than anyone else.

Remember, if you rip off a landlord, and they discover the fact, you might kiss goodbye to their business forever, perhaps rightly too, and quite possibly to all their friends as well.

USEFUL INCOME STREAM

Nevertheless you could build up a very useful additional revenue stream by establishing a repairs and maintenance wing to your business. One agency I knew made more money from their repairs division than they ever did from property management, which might give you a flavour of what could be achieved.

There are never enough companies to go round in this field, especially in times of emergency. For example after severe gales, when there are numerous repair jobs to be picked up, such as tiles blown off and fences down.

If you are running a property management agency you will become embroiled in sorting out maintenance matters, whether you like it or not. Treat the opportunity professionally. Get organised, recruit good quality trades people, pay them promptly, and make sure your time is adequately rewarded.

In time you could expand and develop your maintenance division too, perhaps when property management may be going through a quieter spell. You are not, and never have been, a one trick pony, and this is a real opportunity to create additional income for very little outlay.

Why not look at offering full painting and decorating services? Your landlords will often require work doing on all their property, ranging from a small sprucing up job to a full right through paint exercise. I am not suggesting you do the work yourself! You may well obtain a stream of regular work from this source, and there is good money to be made here too.

Gardening and window cleaning can also pay well, but a little word of warning here. Insurance is very difficult to obtain for any work people who may be scaling ladders, and the last thing you would want would be a big claim from a maintenance person who fell and broke a leg. That doesn't bear thinking about; so do check the insurance angle before you widen your operations in this area.

To recap:

Establish New Revenue Streams
Consider Insurance Policies &
Mortgage Introductions
Reduce Your Utility Bills
Build Up a Network of
Good Maintenance People
Establish Your Own Repairs Division

Nineteen:
Dealing With
Difficult Tenants

Far and away the best way to deal with troublesome tenants is not to have any in the first place. It's a fact of property letting life that providing you have carried out your referencing procedures thoroughly, you will weed out the vast majority of bad tenants. Indeed you might be surprised at how few difficult customers you ever come across.

Nevertheless, sooner or a later, you will land yourself with a problem tenant, the nightmare person you'd always imagined. You can take comfort from the fact that **every agent** does so sooner or later, even the largest and strongest, and very best. There isn't an agent alive who hasn't experienced a bad tenant at some point in their commercial career. If they say they haven't, they're lying. The acid test will be to see how you deal with the problem.

TYPES OF BAD TENANT

Troublesome tenants come in six fishy flavours.

1. The rowdy snapping piranha, who upsets the neighbours
2. The disappearing dogfish, who does a runner
3. The sprat who can't, or won't, pay the rent

4. The destroyer shark, who damages or wrecks the place
5. The moaning marling, who will find fault with everything
6. The barnacle, who downs anchors and refuses to move

The moment you become aware you have a problem with a tenant it is most important to deal with the matter immediately. Don't put it off. If you leave it to fester, more often than not, it will only get worse. So how do you handle problem lets, and problem tenants? Here are a few suggestions.

1. THE NOISY TENANT

If you receive telephoned or written complaints from neighbours about excessive noise, you need to write to the tenant immediately. But before you get all worked up about it and fire off a missive, bear in mind that you only have the neighbour's word regarding the problem, and sometimes neighbours can be as naughty and mischievous as any tenant.

Some neighbours think that people who rent property are beneath them and shouldn't be allowed to live next door in their swanky neighbourhood. Some neighbours will do anything to have renters moved on. Bear that in mind. There are two sides to every story.

Your letter should reflect that possibility. I suggest wording along the lines of: "We have received a complaint (s) regarding excessive noise and late night disturbances. **IF** this is indeed the case, please do all you can to ensure there is no repetition."

The words 'IF THIS IS INDEED THE CASE,' are the most important. Some tenants on receiving such a letter will realise they have been a little noisy, and will keep quieter in the future. Often you'll never hear a thing about it again. But it's more likely they will ring the office looking for a row.

"How dare you write a letter like this accusing me of all sorts", would be a typical riposte, and occasionally a great deal ruder! Develop thick skin. You might need it.

You politely point out that you haven't accused anyone of anything, you clearly said **IF** there was a disturbance. You should then move the conversation on to ask if they heard anything. Was there a problem in the road? Drunks perhaps? Had they been disturbed themselves?

Should you subsequently receive a second complaint, may be from a different source, you have no alternative but to write to the tenant again detailing these further complaints. You may need to state that should there be further problems you may have to take steps to bring the tenancy to an end.

With a little luck the tenancy may well be nearing an end anyway, and if it is coming up for renewal, you, and the landlord, have the handy option of not renewing, and that should solve the problem. Always think very carefully about renewing tenancies with noisy tenants, and if you have to extend, do so for the shortest possible period. In that case the tenancy is running on, in effect, on a further trial basis. Should there be further problems, you could bring it to an early end. Never grant a long-term renewal to a tenant about whom you have received numerous complaints. Move them on instead, and solve the problem that way.

2: MIDNIGHT FLITTERS

The disappearing tenant is a problem, albeit a rare one, but at least they are out of the house. Always try to look at problems from a positive point of view. Never dwell on negatives. Solve the problem by re-letting the property as quickly as possible, so long as the landlord has instructed you so to do. If there is a dilapidation bill for damages incurred, you could try to locate the departed tenant, but you might find that harder than you think.

You could employ an outside agency to try and track them down, but that all costs money. More often than not you would be throwing good money after bad. Consider cutting your losses, that's the advice we would give the landlord, although the total value of any outstanding claim would need to be considered.

Remember too, to examine any valid insurance policies. They may well cover the landlord against midnight flitters and unplanned damage. If the landlord hasn't taken out any insurance, now might be a good time to try and sell them a policy for the future. Remind them of the merits of such a policy. Most landlords will reinvest a little of their rental income in insurance, if you highlight the benefits. So why not through you?

3: NON-PAYERS

The non-payer of rent is always a challenge for any agent, and of course the problem always gets worse during periods of general financial downturn. I go back to the referencing stage again. If the references were good, non-payment of rent is a surprisingly rare event. Yes, sometimes people can be a week or two late, especially if they are sending in cheques, but serious rent arrears are not that common.

Check also to see if there is a guarantor on the contract. If there is, do not hesitate to write or ring the guarantor. Tell them the tenant has not paid, and could they (the guarantor) make a prompt payment to put the matter straight, as is their obligation under the terms of the tenancy agreement. The spectre of an eventual eviction is there, if the guarantor does not put the matter right.

It is their responsibility to do so. It's another good argument for having a guarantor on the contract in the first place. Often when you approach a guarantor about problems it inspires them into kicking the tenant into action. A guarantor can often be a heck of a sight ruder to a tenant than you could ever be!

You need to keep a close eye on all the rents coming in, another reason why standing orders and computerised banking are so desirable. You can immediately see whether the rents are in or not when you run your daily check. If it isn't, ring the tenant and politely ask if there is a problem with the SOM. Ask them to check with the bank and call you back. Sometimes banks won't make a standing order payment for 500.00 if there is only 480.00 in the account. Ask the tenant to bring the full rent to your office as soon as possible to put the matter right.

If another week goes by and the tenant has not corrected the situation it is time for a letter along the lines of, "The rent is still overdue and you have not called in to see us or rung back. Please put the matter right within 7 days, otherwise your tenancy could be at risk".

It always pays dividends to be quite strict with new tenants because it establishes a precedent. If you adopt the opposite line, being lenient with newcomers, they might read it that you are weak. If they do that, things could go downhill quickly.

I have never met a tenant yet who wanted to be evicted and that is the ultimate sanction if they fail to put matters right. Even the merest hint of an eviction rapidly corrects matters in most cases.

Remember, the beauty of an Assured Shorthold Tenancy is that providing the paperwork has been correctly prepared, the court is bound to issue an eviction notice once the tenant has missed two monthly payment dates. If you have a tenant who does not pay, you must keep on at them until the matter is resolved. Don't put it to the back of jobs to do, don't ignore it, treat it as your number one priority, and keep on at it until it is sorted out. Your landlord will appreciate your vigorous efforts. They certainly won't, if you leave the matter unresolved.

If the tenant still does not pay, issue them with a notice requiring possession of the property. You can obtain those from Oyez or find them within any property management program. It's a very rare hard faced tenant who ignores such an order. If the guarantor doesn't pay, threaten them with legal action as well. It's amazing the quick results a solicitor's letter often produces, and they do not cost a fortune.

If the tenant can't or won't co-operate you will need to go to court and obtain an eviction order. This is very rare, believe me, and it is the last thing you want too because it is both costly and time consuming. In ten years I only went to court twice, and on both occasions the tenant left the property before the eviction notice could be issued. Speak to your local court office for advice. They are very helpful and will provide you with the necessary forms to complete, and a free booklet explaining the procedure.

It is not unduly complicated and the court office will always help you to get it right. You don't need to employ a solicitor to do this for you if you don't want to. Simply follow the clear instructions laid out on the forms.

4: DAMAGE TO PROPERTY

Dealing with the destroyer shark of a tenant depends upon how you discovered the damage. You may have noticed problems during a periodic inspection. In that case you should immediately ask the tenant to put matters right. Follow it up with a letter, that way it is recorded on the file. You can tell them that you will return in ten days time to inspect the repairs.

If the damage is discovered when you book the tenant out, you can advise them immediately that there will be a claim against the security deposit to put matters right. The tenant won't like that, but it is their fault and their responsibility. They should have dealt with the matter before the tenancy came to an end. You also have the option of sending a bill to a guarantor, if there is one. You can even invite the guarantor to come and inspect the damage if you feel it might bring matters to a speedy conclusion. Guarantors can and do make good dilapidation bills, and not only that, guarantors can sometimes embarrass tenants into making good damage they have clearly caused.

I had one guarantor who coughed up an unbelievable 17,000.00 for damage that was primarily pet dirt on expensive carpets, rather than face a public court case, and another one who paid 4,000.00 just to bring the matter to a speedy conclusion, and to stop us from pestering him at work. Always be polite, but firm. You are only looking to return the property to the condition it was in before the tenant moved in. You or the landlord should never be trying to make any additional revenue from the incident. If you do that, you will quickly gain a bad reputation in the industry, and you certainly do not want to go in that direction.

Remember:

Guarantors **DO** pay dilapidation bills.
It is a complete myth that they don't.

5: THE MOANER

The complaining tenant is the one I have to confess who annoyed me the most. They can become a real pain in the neck. A professional complainer can be on the phone every other day, yes, as often as that! The water doesn't heat up quickly enough, the garage needs painting, the television reception is poor, the gutters could do with a clean, one of the tiles on the kitchen floor is cracked, and the tree needs pruning, etc, etc, etc. The list is endless. You name it, and the professional complainer can moan about it. We all know people in the general walk of life who are like that.

Don't get me wrong; if there is a genuine maintenance problem, it has to be dealt with as soon as possible, full stop. But there are genuine problems and spurious ones and the professional moaner doesn't seem capable of seeing the difference. You might consider a quiet word in the tenant's ear along the lines of: "Your tenancy is soon to be renewed, isn't it? We don't really want to bother the landlord AGAIN over that, do we?"

This tack often works wonders, and unfortunately, sometimes it is your only option. Use your best judgement. Some people are <u>never</u> satisfied and they will test your patience to the limit, and beyond. It wastes your time, and distracts you from your prime aims.

Personally, if a tenant were continually unreasonable I would recommend to the landlord that the tenancy agreement was not renewed. They could always move out and take a tenancy in one of your competitor's properties. Let your rivals have the hassle. There are plenty of other fishes in the sea, and good ones too.

6: THE NON-MOVER

Lastly, good old Barnacle Bill, the one who downs anchors and refuses to budge. This is the nightmare scenario that landlords always imagine will happen to them. I cannot emphasise enough how rare this is. The ultimate sanction would be for Barnacle and his family of grubby little urchins be visited by bailiffs and ultimately be forcibly removed from the home and dumped in the rain on the lawn outside, together with all their pungent belongings.

Not a pretty sight, I know, and one to be avoided if at all possible, but the tenant knows full well that that will be the final outcome. They would have to be either very stupid or disturbed to follow that route. Believe me, I come back once again to the referencing procedure at the outset; if you have done your job properly, it should never happen. If the tenant has a history of downing anchors, you should have discovered that at the outset, in which case you should not have housed them.

If it gets as far as an eviction order the tenant only have themselves to blame. If they still won't move out voluntarily, recruit the full force of the law to remove them. A contract is a contract. You and the landlord have fulfilled your side to the letter. It is not too much to expect the other party to do so too. They will be evicted. It is as simple as that.

Tenants who don't pay the rent &
Tenants who don't look after the property
are NOT wanted.
Move them on.
Let your competitors enjoy them
Find someone else.

BAD CUSTOMERS

All businesses have the occasional bad customer, for that is what the tenants are, your, and your landlords' customers. What matters is how you deal with them. To do nothing and hope that things will be all right eventually is a terrible policy to adopt. If you have a problem, confront it as early as you can, and sort it out. It will cause you far less grief in the long term.

When you do have a problem with a tenant, it is advisable to keep your landlord fully informed of the difficulty at the earliest opportunity. It is not an easy phone call to make, but it is an important one. The odds are they will understand, they have probably had difficulties themselves in the past. Hopefully they'll simply tell you to: "Get on with it and sort it out. You're the agent, aren't you? It is what we pay you for."

If you leave it for weeks without mentioning a problem to a landlord, it becomes harder and harder to tell them, and when you eventually do, they have the killer question back, "You've known about this for seven weeks and you haven't told me anything about it. Why the heck not?"

They won't be happy, and your relationship could become strained. (Or worse!)

Establish a clear procedure
for dealing with difficult tenants.
Confront problems as soon as possible
Confront problems head on
Put warnings in writing
Keep Landlords Informed

THINGS YOU MUST **NOT** DO

When you do have problems with a tenant there are some things you must <u>never</u> do. You can visit the house to discuss the matter, but you mustn't visit the house threatening people, and you must never employ others to threaten or intimidate. You must never interfere with the supply of services to the house. You must not enter the house and change the locks, and you must not lock the tenant out.

The courts take a very dim view of intimidation, threatening behaviour, and harassment, and rightly so. If you adopt policies such as these, you shift your position from being 100% in the right, with the full force of the law behind you, to being outside the law yourself, and at clear risk of prosecution. There are ways and means of doing things correctly. Never cross the line into illegality. In plain language, never be tempted to "send the boys round!"

Make sure that at all times you operate in the correct manner. Bear in mind that if the matter ever came to court you could be cross-examined, and you certainly do not want to be in the position of admitting any illegal activities or moves.

Never be bullied by over zealous landlords into breaking the law. Some will try to push you into doing so, you can be sure of that. If you have any doubts as to what you are doing and where you stand, speak to your solicitor IMMEDIATELY.

Get to know the law
Stay within the law
Use the law when necessary
Solve problems out of court if possible
Courts cost time and money
Be persistent
Don't lose your temper
Be **professional** at all times

Twenty:
Extending Contracts
& Inspecting Properties

An Assured Shorthold Tenancy agreement should be for a minimum of three months but the usual minimum period is six months. But you can if you wish prepare a contract for two years or even longer. I would not recommend a contract for longer than two years because you are tying the landlord into a fixed rental figure they cannot then increase. Imagine if rampant inflation returned, and who is to say it couldn't?

Much better to grant a shorter term to begin with and once you get to know the tenant better, then you can consider extending it for a longer period.

LIASE WITH BOTH PARTIES

It's a good idea to regularly liase with both the tenant and landlord to discover their thinking with regard to extending contracts. Many tenants will openly tell you if they are planning to leave after six months, or alternatively, that they would like to remain in the house for another year, or longer. A good agent always knows what their tenant's are thinking of, and looking for.

When an initial period expires the tenancy does NOT come to an automatic end, unless the appropriate notice bringing it to an end has been served, or the tenant has confirmed in writing they wish to leave. If no notice has been served, the tenancy relapses to what is called a **Periodic Tenancy.**

This Periodic contract runs on indefinitely until one party or the other brings it to a close. The landlord or agent would need to serve the appropriate notice, which would give the tenant a minimum of two month's notice that the landlord required possession of the property.

On the other side of the coin, you should note that the tenant would only have to give one month's notice IN WRITING, to bring the contract to a close. Either party cannot give notice over the telephone. If a tenant rings the office and says, "I'm giving a month's notice", you **must** ask them to confirm the fact in writing. If you don't have a letter, you have no proof the tenant gave notice, and it wouldn't be the first tenant who changed their mind or told a fib, and denied all knowledge of the telephone conversation.

ISSUING A NOTICE REQUIRING POSSESSION

So it follows that if the landlord requires possession of the property at the end of the six months you MUST issue the appropriate notice after 4 months, in effect giving the tenant 2 month's notice. It is a good idea to do that 7 or 14 day's prior to the cut off point. It's also a very good idea to hand the notice in person to the tenant, or send it by recorded delivery, so you can be certain it has been delivered and received.

Some agents actually issue this notice at the **same** time as signing the initial contract, that way they never forget to do it, and you might consider this to. (Forgetting can cause you big problems.) The forms required are included in the previously mentioned Oyez forms package or can be found in most property software programs. They are short and very easy to complete. Alternatively, you can also download the necessary notices and indeed any other forms to do with letting property at **www.lawpack.co.uk**

If you are going to issue the notice requiring repossession after four months of a six months tenancy you should diarise the date. You could write a large note on the file when you start any let, of the date when you know that notice needs to be given. If you flipped through the files every week you will keep abreast of which tenancies are approaching the cut-off point. Or better still; diarise the fact in your daily diary so you can't forget it, then liase with the landlord. Good agents always have an idea of their landlords and tenants thinking regarding the period beyond the tenancy, for ALL their lets. Do you?

A FURTHER FIXED TERM

Once the initial contract is approaching an end, and is due to revert to that Periodic Tenancy the landlord may feel uneasy that the tenant could simply give a month's notice and quit. The way around that is to issue a Memorandum extending the existing contract for a further fixed term. You do **not** need to prepare a whole new tenancy agreement.

Bear in mind it's in your best interests too. If you have a satisfactory letting proceeding without any problems at say 750.00 per month, you could be retaining 75.00 of that every month. If you can extend the contract for another year, you are locking in another 900.00 of guaranteed minimum revenue.

If the property became empty, anything might happen. The landlord might give the house to another agent for one, they could sell it for another, or move into it themselves, or give it to their son or daughter, or you might struggle to let it again. These are all great incentives for you, and the landlord, if rental income is paramount, to keep the tenant in the property, and the best way to do that, is to have both parties sign an early extension.

The Memorandum should simply refer to the original tenancy agreement, listing the start date, and the parties involved. It should state, "The tenancy has been extended for a further 6 months (or whatever figure you like, up to 24) and will now end on June 26th 2009 (or whatever the date is). All other terms and conditions remain unchanged."

You could also consider a rent increase at this time too, providing you don't frighten the tenant away. If an increase is agreed, simply incorporate that fact in the Memo. Don't be too greedy on increases, and advise landlords to think that way too. If the increase was too much and the property came empty and then stayed empty for a period of say, two or three months, imagine the total rental missed, revenue that is lost forever, both for you and the landlord and it may be for the sake of 20.00 or so. Swingeing rent increases are a sure way to aggravate tenants, and you can expect to be sitting on an increasing numbers of empty properties if you become too greedy.

Remember too, to amend any standing order mandates if you bump up the rent. Prepare the Memo in duplicate, have both parties sign, and send a signed copy to each party. Take a photocopy too and stick it in your file and remember to diarise it again for when the contract is next due to be renewed or reviewed.

Always bear in mind your prime target, and that is to keep your properties **full** (with good tenants) and under your full management. That is the way to build up substantial residual income.

CHARGING FOR EXTENSIONS

Some agents charge for this service, others don't, relying on the fact they have locked in the existing contract for another fixed term in the sure knowledge they have protected their revenue for another year or so. We charged a small fee, 40.00, and so long as it was listed in your original Fact Pack, you are quite within your rights to charge for this service if you so wish. If you do, you've created another revenue stream for yourself. That's what it's all about. Creating revenue, because ultimately, creating revenue gives you power.

PROPERTY INSPECTIONS

Inspecting properties during the tenant's stay is an important duty you should carry out. Some landlords absolutely insist on regular inspections of all their properties, especially the more nervous ones, landlords that is, but some landlords don't give a hoot whether you inspect or not. Indeed there is an argument that says that too frequent inspections may unsettle a good tenant and they may up sticks and move away.

Neither you nor your landlord can just roll up at the property without notice and demand to be let in to carry out an on-the-spot inspection. The contract states that the tenant should have "quiet enjoyment" of the property and obviously an on-the-spot unannounced inspection is not within the spirit of the let.

When an inspection is due, write to the tenant and say: "Under the terms of the tenancy we are required to carry out an inspection of the property and we intend to do this at 10am next Thursday 24/07/08. If this is not a convenient time, please ring our office and arrange an alternative appointment".

I would always give a tenant between five and seven days notice before the appointment. We can all be untidy at times, and how would you like people turning up with little or no notice to inspect your house? I know I wouldn't.

Additionally, if the tenant has broken or damaged some items in the house, it gives them a good opportunity to fix it before you arrive. That is fair enough. The chances are they will ring up, whether they want to change the date or not. Usually they will simply ask what it's all about, especially if you have not inspected before. All you need answer is that you are periodically obliged to check things over to make sure everything is all right.

You can reassure them it is normal practice and that it won't take very long.

INSPECTING PROPERTIES

On the day of the inspection arrive at the house on time and be cheerful. Try not to act like the hated teacher at school who crept round the class trying to find fault with everything he could. Make notes as you go round and if there is anything you see that needs dealing with, you could mention it there and then.

Childrens' writing on walls and wallpaper is a common complaint, new stains on the carpets, anything that catches your eye, you have the opportunity to point it out to the tenant and hint that they need to sort it. Remember, if they don't do anything to correct the situation they may be hit in the pocket via a claim against the security deposit when the tenancy comes to a close. It is in the tenant's best interest to keep the property up to standard.

Inspect every room, and outside the property too. Has the lawn been cut? That is the tenant's responsibility. If they haven't done so, it will need to be done. If you don't feel comfortable asking the tenant to carry out certain tasks there and then, you could return to the office and write them a polite letter pointing out your findings and asking them to put the matter straight.

In my experience it is preferable to have a friendly chat and point things out while you are there, than write a letter a few days later. No matter how well worded a letter may be, sometimes the tone may come across as harsh and confrontational. Remember, you are not aiming to upset the tenant; you are simply endeavouring to ensure that the tenancy is being conducted in a satisfactory manner for all parties.

Indeed, the tenant may well take the opportunity to point out various maintenance jobs that need addressing too that are possibly the landlord's responsibility. Perhaps some guttering is leaking, or a fence has blown down. When you return to the office, prepare your report as soon as possible while it is fresh in the memory, and keep a copy on file as proof you have carried out an inspection, and mail the original to the landlord. DO NOT send a copy to the tenant.

Problems solved during routine inspections often go a long way to eradicating difficulties that may arise at the end of the tenancy, so treat it seriously and prepare the ground for a trouble free end to that particular let.

If the landlord has been unaware of the impending inspection they may well be pleased to receive your report out of the blue. It will reinforce in their mind how well you are doing your job, which you are. They may also discuss with you carrying out maintenance jobs, as recommended by your goodselves, and that could mean additional possible revenue for you too, so it hasn't been a complete waste of time, financially speaking. It is in everyone's ultimate interest that all properties are maintained to a high standard.

HOW OFTEN SHOULD INSPECTIONS BE CARRIED OUT?

That's a difficult question to answer. As previously mentioned some landlords don't care about inspections at all. It may seem strange, but it's true. Others would have an inspection carried out every week if they could!

You will have discussed with your landlords their thoughts on the matter. Some tenants need to be inspected more regularly than others, some very rarely, others regularly, and you will soon become an expert at deciding which. Some tenants will do everything they can to stop you inspecting the property too. In that case you should ask yourself, why?

If that occurs you should persist in your request for a suitable appointment. If a tenant consistently puts you off, you might consider calling at the house unannounced. If the tenant is in they might let you in, but more likely, they will give you an appointment to call back later. You can point out that under the terms of the agreement they are bound to grant you access. They are breaking the terms of the contract if they consistently deny you entry.

As previously mentioned, neither you nor the landlord may enter the property at anytime without the tenant being present, unless you have the tenant's clear permission to do so, or a court order. Some landlords, especially the amateurs find this very difficult to adhere to. They might say: "This was my late mother's house and I'll go in and check whenever I like". But they can't.

Never be railroaded into entering a house with a landlord unless you have extraordinarily good reasons to do so. For example, if you thought the tenant was seriously ill. You always need a valid reason to enter a let property; and to be on the safe side it might be an idea to ask a policeman to accompany you, especially if you have reason to believe that someone may be ill.

ENTERING HOUSES WITHOUT PERMISSION

I had one landlord who couldn't stop himself entering his property in the afternoon, presumably when he thought the tenant would be at work. One day the tenant came home early and found him standing there in the middle of the sitting room.

"What the hell are you doing here?" yelled the furious woman.
"I just thought I'd let myself in, to see that everything was all right."
"Oh did you now? Well take that!" The tenant was so livid; she slapped him hard about the face and hustled him from the building.

Later on, she rang me in a fury and refused from that point onward to pay any further rental until she received a written apology and an assurance that no one would ever enter the house again without her knowledge. Fact is, the landlord could have been there to steal the tenant's possessions, he wasn't, but he could have been. No excuse for slapping him though. That was clearly out of order too.

Some landlords need guidance and expertise. Many things are a matter of common sense. Remember, once the landlord signs that tenancy agreement they no longer has the same rights and uses over the property as they had before. That is precisely what the tenant is paying for, so if you ever feel that the landlord is overstepping the mark; don't be afraid to politely point out the dangers. In the longer term they will thank you for it, or at least they jolly well should do.

Be aware of tenants and landlords thinking before tenancy agreements expire

**Carry out Inspections as required
Never enter properties uninvited without the tenant's permission, or a Court Order**

Twenty-One:
Booking Tenants Out

As the end of the tenancy approaches, ring the tenant and make an appointment to meet them at the property to book them out, when hopefully they will have removed all their belongings from the house.

With regard to their removal arrangements, you will need to remain somewhat flexible regarding the time, as removal companies, or departing tenants themselves, don't always finish when they say they will. When you make the appointment impress upon them how important it is that the property should be returned in the same condition it was when let to them. (Allowing for fair wear and tear.)

Remind the tenant too that the house should be thoroughly cleaned, especially if pets have been in the property. You can also politely point out that should the property not be returned in the same neat and tidy condition, the landlord could seek an allowance against the security deposit to cover appropriate cleaning costs and make good any damage.

TASKS TO BE COMPLETED ON BOOKING OUT DAY:

When you attend the property you will need to carry out the following duties:

- Inspect for any damage, if there is any, note it, and point it out to the tenant
- Note down the utility meter readings
- Check the inventory for missing or damaged contents
- Note down the tenant's forwarding address for any future correspondence
- Advise the utility companies where to post their final bills
- Collect ALL the keys issued to the tenant
- Remind the tenant to arrange for the forwarding of their mail
- Let the tenant out of the house, and lock the door behind them. The tenant should NOT re-enter the property again at any time thereafter without your permission
- Place a to-let sign, if you have been instructed to re-let the property, in the front window with the telephone number clearly visible
- Remind the tenant to cancel the standing order mandate. You **cannot** do that for them, and it's surprising how many people forget

RETURNING TENANTS' DEPOSITS

Liase with the landlord as to whether any claim is to be made against the security deposit. If there is, prepare it in writing and advise the tenant accordingly and make a claim to the Deposit holding scheme. The tenant will then either accept it, or dispute the claim. Photographs and written information can often help solve disputes of this nature. You, as the agent, always abide by the terms of the contract, and it is not too much to expect tenants to do the same.

Return to the office and write to the utility companies, as you did when you introduced the tenant. This time of course you are advising them that the tenant has been booked out, that their new address is such and such and that the closing meter reading is XXXXXXX. The utility companies will then send their final bills for that tenant to the new address.

There are some agencies (and landlords too) who have gained a reputation for almost never agreeing that deposits be returned without a fight. Yes, they might gain some additional cash in the short term by making spurious or nit-picking claims but in my view this is a very short-sighted policy.

You are in this business for the long haul and there is nothing to be gained from being unnecessarily confrontational, unless you simply enjoy rows. Even if you are building up the business purely to sell on at a later date, you don't want to be handing over a business that no one ever has a good word to say about. Think "goodwill" not "badwill". No one will want to buy a business weighed down with years and years of sour and mean baggage when it comes to your exit strategy.

Some landlords will want to inspect the properties themselves prior to the matter being put to bed, and that is their prerogative.

PROCESSING DILAPIDATION CLAIMS

If there is a claim for damage, for example a toilet seat is broken and missing, or a newly broken window is discovered on an internal front door, it should be done quickly. If the claim is not agreed, the Deposit holding scheme will intervene and arbitrate, and make a decision as to whether the claim is justifiable, or not. The deposit will be then be returned by them to whichever party they see fit.

In many ways this is far preferable to the old system where often the agent would be forced into making a decision themselves as to how much and to whom the deposit was returned. In those cases all too often all the agent did was make an enemy of both sides. Now that decision has been taken from the agents' hands, and the agent can now genuinely sympathise with any aggrieved party by saying, "It wasn't my decision, you understand."

Try and avoid disputes and arbitration proceedings happening by encouraging all parties to settle amicably. It is only money after all, and often ridiculously small amounts at that, and certainly not worth making an enemy for life over.

Occasionally you will lose a landlord because they feel you did not obtain sufficient of the security deposit to cover damage, real or imaginary, to their property, and so be it. Your conscience is quite clear if you have done everything by the book. It is far better to lose one now and again, than be dragged through the courts over what you judge to be a spurious claim. The vast majority of landlords are fair and reasonable people, just like you and me. Most simply want their monthly rental payment in order they can pay off any outstanding mortgage or to maintain their Spanish villas.

Advise landlords they could face court action if they persist with an unjustifiable claim. Remember too, the best way to take the landlord's mind off claiming a few quid for a missing set of cheap tumblers is to let the property again, as quickly as possible, and preferably at an increased rent. That often works wonders!

And here's another thing. When it comes to dilapidation disputes it isn't unusual in the heat of the moment for tempers to become frayed, very frayed indeed, and occasionally people say things they might later regret. Often the next day, after a good night's sleep (or a sleepless night!) things appear totally different.

Try not to let these issues cloud your thinking. There is little point in wasting a lot of time and brainpower over a missing washing up bowl worth 99p, when you should be concentrating on how and when you are going to re-let the property.

DON'T LEAVE PROPERTIES EMPTY

Bear in mind that the longer any property remains empty, the more likely it is that the landlord will instruct another agent to let it, and consequently, the more likely it is, that you will lose it. Property Instructions to any letting agent are their life-blood. The last thing you want to do is lose the house to BONE'S HOMES up on the hill. Any house, that is. Fight that scenario tooth and nail.

You should be letting these properties too, long before the competition, because you had more than a head's start over them. To begin with, you knew the property was coming empty long before they did, and you should have been advertising and promoting it for at least three weeks before the tenant left.

Any good agent would already have someone lined up for it. You ARE a good agent, because you are always thinking ahead, on the ball, anticipating events. Once you have a good property on your books you must do everything in your power to retain it. If you keep the landlord sweet it is not unusual to retain a house for ten, fifteen, even twenty years. Plenty of retained properties produce plenty of profit for you.

When a house comes empty and you lose it to one of your rivals, you should ask yourself why it happened. And more than that, you should redouble your efforts to make sure it doesn't happen again. Try and take one back from them if you can, even up the score. How does that phrase go? Don't get angry – get even! Yes, that is about right.

THE CHANGEOVER DAY CAN BE A STRESSFUL TIME

The whole process of moving house and booking tenants in and out of properties can be a stressful business for all parties involved. It is a quite complicated affair and all sorts of things can and do go wrong.

It might bucket down all day, the removal men could be late, or not turn up at all, the tenant might not appear, or their children might have fallen sick, or may be they are simply not ready to move out, or in. The electricity or gas might not be on (as was arranged), an essential repair that a potential tenant previously pointed out, might not have been carried out, despite you arranging for it to be done. These things happen, and much more besides. Expect the unexpected.

No matter what the difficulty is, the secret is to keep calm, remain cheerful and positive. Don't lose your temper. Always remain helpful and seemingly in control. That calmness will spread to others. You have done it hundreds of times before, even if you haven't!

Never become tetchy and agitated, leave that for others; and no matter how much you may dislike a particular individual, do not let it show or let it become personal. Treat everyone with your same professional manner and you will be fine.

Landlords occasionally attend the move in/out day, even though they have employed you to look after such matters, and unfortunately some of them can't resist making the changeover day more difficult than it might otherwise be. Sometimes they become incredibly tense seeing imaginary difficulties everywhere, and that is all the more reason for YOU to remain calm and in control. That very tenseness is contagious. Cool heads always deal with matters better than hot heads. It seems so simple and straight forward when you think about it. It makes you wonder why everyone doesn't see matters in the same light. But unfortunately they don't.

Remind yourself if necessary that your main goal is to return to the office as soon as possible and concentrate on your letting business, not just that house, but dozens of other properties too.

Booking tenants out is a necessary chore, but NEVER let it take up more of your thinking time, your professional time, than is absolutely necessary.

Always try to:

Remain calm
Remain cheerful
Remain helpful
Set a good example
Rise above tensions
Get the job done
Get away!

Twenty-Two:
Tax, Tax, and Tax Again

The taxman! What a blessed subject! Don't we all just love the guy? When you first start DENT'S RENTS you should tell the Inland Revenue that you have commenced in the lettings business as an agent. You are obliged to do so, and should do so, after all, it's not as if they can send you a tax bill when you first start your business.

It may be tempting not to bother, but sooner or later they will become aware of your activities and they will be mighty miffed if you haven't advised them. Start as you mean to go on, do things by the book, and tell them where you are, and what you are doing.

THE VATMAN

You have no need to register for VAT until your turnover of fees (not rents) rises to above £67,000 per annum (at the time of writing. (Your local VAT office will confirm if that figure has changed.) But keep a careful eye on your turnover figure as it increases, because sooner or later you will approach and bust that figure, and the VATMAN takes no prisoners when they discover traders who have exceeded the threshold and are still unregistered.

I freely admit I made that mistake myself and when the VAT inspector came and looked through our books he was able to show that we had exceeded the threshold by a measly 180.00 ten months before we actually thought we had. This resulted in us receiving a VAT bill for the missing ten months for ALL the VAT that we should have charged to our clients on our fees.

We couldn't pass on those additional costs retrospectively for work done months before. Technically we might have been able to, but it would have been such a PR nightmare we bit our tongue and stood the bill. I thought the VAT office was being particularly mean, but all the guy said as he smiled was: "It's nothing personal, it's only money, pity really." Yeah it was. We'd made a silly mistake, albeit an honest one, and paid for it handsomely. Make sure that you don't.

Someone told me that VAT inspectors are paid commission on any additional VAT they can dig up. I don't know if that's true, and I'm sure they'd deny it, but if it is, I think it should be stopped, because it makes them over zealous. Just my opinion.

The TAX communities are the one institution in the country that does not have to prove you guilty of an offence. In any tax investigation the onus is on you to prove your innocence. This is incredibly difficult to do. If the taxman says: "I think you have drawn 2,000.00 cash out of the business that you have not declared", how the heck do you prove you otherwise?

So make sure you register for VAT in good time. Incidentally, at the time of writing, residential rents are

NOT subject to VAT, though I wonder how long that will remain the case. As we all know, the treasury do not need too many invitations to dream up a new tax or two.

So though there is no necessity to charge VAT on rents, all your agency fees certainly are vatable, once you break the threshold, so you will need to charge your clients VAT at the rate prevailing at the time, (presently 17.5% on top of your fees).

On a 1,000.00 per month let, where you are taking 10% commission, your monthly fee of 100.00 would then be subject to VAT. Assuming the rate is the same, the VAT chargeable and subsequently payable to the VAT office would be 17.50. So it follows that where the landlord was suffering a 100.00 monthly deduction from their rent before you were registered for VAT, the total deduction would now increase to 117.50 after you have registered.

You can clearly see from this example why landlords will prefer to deal with you <u>before</u> you are registered, because they will receive more money; it's as simple as that. If in any doubt, consult your accountant who will clarify all VAT matters for you.

OVERSEAS LANDLORDS TAX LIABILITY

The third taxman you will need to keep a close eye on involves overseas landlords. You might think it would be unusual to have an overseas landlord, but with so many Britons now living abroad, especially in France, Greece,

Spain and Portugal, not to mention the United States, overseas landlords are becoming very common indeed.

The important point to bear in mind here is that unless you have an approval number from the local Inland Revenue Overseas Residents Department to pay the rental in full to the landlord, you, as the agent will become liable for tax on that income. If you don't have an approval number you should deduct 23% (this rate fluctuates with tax rates, and it might be an idea to check the current rate with the Overseas Residents Dept) from the rental and retain it ready for paying over to the Revenue. They will send you an annual or quarterly returns form, which on completion shows the total rent collected on each property, and the total tax that YOU, as the responsible collecting agent, must pay to the Revenue. Go here for bags more information: www.hmrc.gov.uk/cnr/nr_landlords.htm

Of course you are being used again as an unpaid tax collector, and we all know there is nothing new in that. There is also nothing you can do about it. If you sent a bill to the Chancellor's office for the time you spent on tax collecting tasks I think we would all know the outcome of that. Once you have an approval number for each landlord, you simply list that number on the annual return and the matter should be closed. You can then pay the landlord their rent in full, after your fees of course.

If you paid all the rent money, say 8,000.00 in a given year without making any tax deductions, to an owner who is basking in the Greek sunshine, and the Revenue then asked you to pay 23% of it back to them, you

255

wouldn't be very happy. In my experience the vast majority of landlords receive an approval number without any difficulty and most overseas residents who rent out property are well aware of this system and their obligations.

It should not come as a nasty surprise to them, but don't ever let them browbeat you into releasing all of the cash by saying, "It'll be all right, if at a later date there's ever a problem, we can always reimburse you". I don't think so. You are obliged to deduct the tax at source if you haven't a number, that is the system, that is the law, and that is all there is to it.

It could be that the landlord already knows they are not entitled to an approval number, for whatever reason, in which case you will eventually be landed with the bill. Without an approval number, it won't be "All right". Don't ever fall into this chasm of a mistake. Get it right from the beginning and you will have a stress free life when it comes to overseas landlords' tax. You might earn a little extra interest too, as the deducted money for the taxman remains on deposit in your clients' bank account until the payment to the Revenue office becomes due. That is the least you deserve in my humble opinion.

LIASE WITH THE REVENUE

If you have any problems with property revenue taxes speak to your local Inland Revenue office; they will soon put you through to the right department. Ask them to send you the relevant booklets and forms to apply for approval numbers. It is not a huge tome like some of the other stuff they send out. It is simply written and easy to follow, and if you still have a problem with it, ring them up and ask for assistance and advice. You may be pleasantly surprised how eager they are to help. They'll supply you with all the free pamphlets you need that you can hand to your landlords from the outset. You could even incorporate them into your Fact Pack.

Should one of your existing landlords suddenly move abroad you would also need to start making that 23% deduction immediately until an approval number is issued. No approval number means: **No full rental payment to the overseas based landlord**, full stop. Remember, the Revenue Office will always ask YOU to pay over this money, regardless of whether you have deducted it or not, and they will not accept any excuses, particularly feeble ones along the lines of "I've only just started in business and I didn't really know". Ignorance of the law is no defence. It never has been and never will be. Don't be caught out.

To Recap:
For Valued Added Tax
Don't Forget to Register in Time
Your Fees are Vatable once you reach the threshold
Residential Rents are NOT subject to VAT
The Threshold Figure Regularly Changes
Keep Aware of it
Overseas Landlords Rent **is** Taxable
Unless you have an Approval Number
The Agent is Responsible for Retaining and Paying
That Tax to the Revenue Office

Twenty-Three:
I Don't Want to be an Estate Agent!

Well of course you don't, after all aren't estate agents consistently ranked alongside traffic wardens as the profession the general public most love to hate? (An unjustified reputation in my humble opinion, as almost all of the estate agents I have ever known have been hard working and conscientious). Perhaps I have just been lucky.

But as you become a more established and successful letting and management agent, I guarantee that you will start to glance enviously at your estate agent cousins. Why? Money of course. If an estate agent sells a single property worth 300,000 even on the lower bands of 1% commission, that agent would earn at least 3,000.00 on that one deal. It takes a large number of lets and hard work to earn 3,000.00 in letting revenue.

Contrary to the popular view, I don't think an estate agent does more work on a single transaction than a letting agent. Do they have to read meters, write to services, check inventories, reference tenants, prepare a legal tenancy agreement, and collect deposits? No, they don't, most don't even bother to accompany viewers. So I guess it's natural that a letting agent should look at the estate agents' large commission with more than simply an envious eye.

CONSIDERING ESTATE AGENCY

Even if you have no intention of ever becoming an estate agent, I can guarantee certain circumstances will arise that will at the very least make you think more than once about it. The property letting and management business like so many industries runs in cycles. Some months you will be rushed off your feet, but in quieter times you will suddenly find some time on your hands.

January and September are invariably busy months for lettings, as indeed they are for many businesses. The children have gone back to school, and many employed people are starting new jobs and new employment contracts, often away from their hometowns. Many of these people decide to retain their own homes and rent a second property to be close to their new workplace.

The property letting business can also be affected by changing house prices. When prices are low and depressed and sales are slow moving, a great deal more property floods on to the lettings market. Perhaps some landlords and property owners suddenly have negative equity, where even if they wanted to sell, they are debarred from doing so, unless they are prepared to make good the shortfall in equity.

Perhaps sales are not moving too well and to avoid the property standing empty, many property owners will turn to the lettings market, and rent out, if only for a short time, to cover their mortgage payments. They'll do this until prices and demand picks up again. This can be a very successful time for letting agents because there will be an almost unlimited number of properties available to be let out. Grab them while they're there, as many as you can, and lock them into decent length contracts which protects your forward income.

THOSE MONDAY MORNING CALLS

But when property prices move up sharply, some of these landlords will, possibly for the very first time, see the opportunity to bale out, to make a fat juicy profit, and many will do just that. Horribly, they often come together in batches of five and six houses at a time, and usually from completely unconnected landlords, and when you least expect it. You experience the rush of those Monday morning telephone calls along the lines of: "I've been thinking over the weekend". And you wonder what's coming next, and then they hit you.

Your friendly landlord, the same person for whom you have worked so hard to please, and who, you could be forgiven for thinking, would remain with you for years and years to come, suddenly tells you that they have grown tired of the letting game, as they often refer to it, and are selling up. Oh dear! Not what you want to hear at all. Sometimes they will cursorily add: "You don't do SALES do you?"

You confirm the fact, glum faced, indeed you don't do sales, and the next thing you know, those four fine hugely coveted houses suddenly appear in the much-maligned   Snodgrass   and   Company's   fine advertisement, <u>FOR SALE</u>.

You glance at the asking prices, 150,000, 200,000, 250,000 and 300,000 and you snort and think they'll never sell them at those prices! They are wasting their time!

But suddenly the market is moving up again. The buyers are back in droves, and within three weeks all four properties have incredibly sold. They will <u>never</u> appear on the rental market ever again, and you curse aloud. Your mind goes into overdrive, and you begin to think about all that commission, that money, and you wonder about how you could increase YOUR fees.

You quickly work out in your head that those four houses sold for the thick end of 900,000 and even on just 1% commission; old Snodgrass has just trousered nine grand, for three week's work! Nine grand! That's a heck of a lot of rental commissions. How many houses would you have to rent, and manage, and for how long, to make nine grand? A single house earning you 50.00 per month commission would have to be rented out for fifteen straight years to make nine flipping grand! And he's pocketed it, the slimy Snodgrass, in a week!

And worse even than that, old Snodgrass has twenty-two more to come, judging by his ever-growing advertisement of colourful properties FOR SALE, and you think, Heck! What is going on here? What is to stop me SELLING HOUSES TOO?

The answer is:

NOTHING! ABSOLUTELY NOTHING!

NO LICENCE IS REQUIRED

At the time of writing you do NOT need a licence to set up an estate agency business in England and Wales. You cannot do so if you have been made bankrupt, or if the Office of Fair Trading informs you that you must not. They might take that course of action if they hold numerous complaints on their files about the way you have conducted your business affairs in the past, another good reason to run a straight and honest ship in the first place. There are continuing calls for regulation of the industry, but as yet, none have been forthcoming, though this is something that you would need to keep a sharp eye on.

Other than that, you CAN, though you MUST be fully aware that the legalities of trading as an estate agency are entirely different to that of being a letting agent.

(In the United Sates you do need a licence and you need to pass the Real Estate Exam. You can find out all about that at http://www.dre.ca.gov/ and you can also look at www.hud.gov for more US information.)

For a start you have to rigidly comply with the Trade Descriptions Act of 1968, but much more importantly with the Estate Agency Act of 1979, and most especially the Property Misdescriptions Act of 1991. To fail to do so could land you in serious and expensive trouble. For British readers please check out the website www.oft.gov.uk and look at the huge sections dealing with estate agency.

Here are just three simple examples of where you could run into trouble.

Firstly, if you included room measurements on your property particulars and were just six inches out, you could be prosecuted by the Office of Fair Trading or indeed by a potential property buyer, even if it was a genuine typing error by your new young typist. An accidental mistake is no defence. It is a mistake, and it could be a very costly one. Fines can run into huge figures, so it's best to get professional indemnity insurance. You could even be de-barred from trading overnight. Not a happy thought.

Secondly, if you sell a property you own, or one belonging to a relative, you are legally obliged to include that fact prominently within the sales particulars. If you didn't, the same penalties could also be imposed.

Thirdly, if you displayed a property in a window display at 200,000 but inside your shop, or office, or in one of your advertisements you had reduced it to 190,000 and had forgotten to amend your other displays; you could once again be falling foul of the Acts and could face surprisingly severe penalties. I am not trying to put you off the idea, but rather to steer you well clear of the many slippery crevasses that lie strewn across your path.

Then there is the HIP Pack saga. Home Information Packs are now compulsory for all sellers on any properties in the United Kingdom, and you would need to do your homework on that one too. Google "HIP

Packs" and you will be inundated with more information and advice you can shake a stick at.

But if you are interested in developing your business into estate agency, study the ramifications of the Acts, speak to your trade associations, check out the myriad of information that is available on the internet, teach yourself all there is to know, and ultimately, you will be well equipped to set up your own sales division.

And the next time there's a rush of properties leaving the rental sector and a landlord says to you: "You don't do sales do you?" You can reply smiling, "But of course we do, we'll get right on it."

NO ONE IS BETTER PLACED TO START

You are in an excellent position to do so too, because you have a register of landlords just waiting for your attention. You could even mail shot them all, something along the lines of:

THINKING OF SELLING? – LOOK NO FURTHER!

You could offer a special deal to your long-term clients, and don't forget too, that you may well have professional clients and landlords looking to BUY property, to expand their own property portfolios.

You could try and match them, to produce quick sales, at low cost to yourself. You could pocket the commission for selling a property; yet still have the opportunity to rent it out for the new owners. What could be better? Use your imagination, the potential is limitless.

YOU **DON'T** NEED A SHOP

Contrary to popular opinion you don't need a shop to sell property. Many real estate agents in the USA don't have a shop, they carry out their entire operation from office-based accommodation, and there are many more businesses doing precisely the same thing in Britain and Australia. It is becoming quite common, and there are good reasons to do so.

A display advertisement with a good photograph in your local newspaper is your shop window, along with the Internet of course, and that is all you really need. The only person who won't appreciate your new enterprise is old Snodgrass of course, and you don't owe him a living. Would he help you out with additional rental properties when your market was quiet? Fat chance!

Here's another thought too. During the past ten or twelve years a huge number of new independent estate agencies have opened up from Tenerife to Tottenham, from Miami to Manchester and seemingly all stops in between. In recent months with property prices turning downward, quite a few of these new independents have lost a little interest and some have started to sell up and get out of the industry. If house prices continue to fall you can expect to see more people looking to cut and run.

Why is that so interesting? Because it produces opportunities, that's why. Some of these people simply want out, some are <u>desperate</u> to get out, and many have cut their asking prices to achieve it. If you are serious about looking at estate agency, pick up a copy of Dalton's Weekly. That is the paper that specialises in selling businesses. It comes out every Thursday and inside you will probably find some estate agents for sale, and some of them will be very attractively priced too. Check out their website too at: www.daltons.co.uk

I have recently seen some agencies for sale at a figure far less than it would cost to buy a shop lease and refurbish the premises. The beauty of buying an established business is that you not only acquire ready equipped premises, but also a healthy register of properties ready to go. A good register of properties equates to early potential income, and combined with what you have already built up yourself, this could give your business a massive shot in the arm. In many cases you might not need to take the shop, if you don't want to. Occasionally the value of the existing property register is worth more than the asking price alone.

If you are ever tempted to buy an established business make sure that you are not taking on any of their previous, possibly hidden debts, or any VAT liability either, or any liability for uncollected rental on properties they may have managed. Again, your accountant will advise you on the more intricate details to do with purchasing an ongoing business, and don't scrimp in this area.

If you are interested in branching into estate agency and have the necessary capital to do so, consider acquiring an established business because there is good value to be had when sellers are keen to get out. And when you find something to suit, remember to haggle aggressively over the price. The sellers are advertising their businesses for sale because they want out, they want to sell; they may need to sell, sometimes at almost any price. You, as a buyer, are giving them that precious exit strategy, and perhaps no one else will, so make sure you strike the best deal you possibly can.

Incidentally, property management and letting does not come under the scope of the Estate Agents Act, but as I have mentioned before, it is a very good idea to study and gain a qualification both for lettings and sales. Sooner or later, I am certain this will become a statutory requirement. It will also impress your clients and induce confidence in you as a professional person, when they notice you're signing correspondence with the appropriate letters after your name. It's not as hard to achieve as you might imagine.

Of course you do not have to buy an existing estate agency to begin selling property for your clients. You could simply start by including some property **for sale** in your existing advertising, perhaps as a test marketing operation. And why shouldn't you? There is no reason. Just make sure you do your homework thoroughly before you launch.

<u>BUT I DON'T WANT TO BE AN ESTATE AGENT...</u>

Well of course you don't. Protest away. But would you like an additional 20,000 earnings EVERY MONTH? Yes? Well, you now know where that could possibly be found. Eight sold properties at 250,000 each on 1% commission would produce 20,000 in fees. And that is for the month! It is not impossible, it really isn't.

One last point on this topic: Imagine for a moment if you earned an extra 20,000 per month. That would provide you with the necessary deposits to buy a new property for rental <u>EVERY MONTH</u>. That equates to twenty-four houses in two years and that is a sizeable portfolio in anyone's language. Don't get me wrong, I am not suggesting you do this straight away, I am not suggesting you walk before you can run, but I am planting the seed in your mind as to where your business could POSSIBLY develop somewhere in the future. Keep an open mind. Nothing is written in stone. You could do it, if you really wanted to.

<u>OR PERHAPS LOOK AT THIS INSTEAD</u>

Is there an independent estate agent on your patch who does not do lettings? There probably is somewhere. Why not approach them with a view to forging a co-operative agreement along the lines of when you have properties for sale you will pass them to them, and when they have properties to rent or contacts with new landlords, they will pass them to you. Agree on some kind of shared commission and this could work well for both parties. They might even let you put up some of your rental details in their shop displays. Be bold and ask, they can only say no.

Twenty-Four:
Acquiring Property

Imagine that you have worked incredibly hard and have scrimped and saved enough cash to put down a deposit on your first buy-to-let property. You didn't have any capital to begin with, nor have you been left money by other people, you've had to do it all the hard way, by yourself, off your own back. Now you are ready to buy your first buy-to-let property, but where are you going to buy it?

As we hinted in the previous chapter, the first place to look is within your own sphere of business activities.

Ask yourself this: Are any of your landlords looking to sell up? If they are, ring them up, or better still, go and see them, find out what they are thinking. Their properties are almost perfect for you, because you know them so well; they are probably tenanted with first class tenants that you have introduced, and the chances are, they have been well maintained following your regular inspections. But if there isn't anything immediately available within your sphere of influence, or you can't afford them, where do you look after that?

One place you should be extremely careful about becoming involved in is via the business opportunity columns in the Sunday newspapers. There has been a huge rise in the number of these companies offering to buy properties (with your money) and manage them for you. What on earth would you need another management agency for? Aren't you by now one of the best agents around?

But, you might say, the properties look **so** cheap with a guaranteed discount. Yes they do, on the face of it, but they are cheap for a reason, and that reason is probably because no one wants to live in them. Let me ask you a question. Would you buy a car without seeing it? Or a house for you to live in, or even a television set? Without examining it? The answer is obviously no, so why would anyone in their right mind consider buying a house for rental purposes without even seeing it? The answer is, because the proposition looks so good. What is it they say? If a proposition looks too good to be true, it probably is.

The houses that are being touted around are often Victorian and Edwardian terraces that are coming to the end of their natural life. Some of them may even be scheduled to be demolished. Alternatively, they are quite likely to be poorly built early 1960's council houses or flats on sprawling estates, many of which contain asbestos, where no one now wants to live, and where the few remaining tenants are desperate to get away from.

Thirdly, they could be modern purpose built flats that are often over-priced to enable a false discount to be built into the asking price. In Lymington in Hampshire a year ago there were apartments being offered for sale at 300,000 where the developer was giving a 15,000 sweetener cheque to buyers who could move in straight away. A year later the sweetener cheques had vanished, but the asking prices on the flats had dropped to 230,000. (This is before the great crunch!)

There have been a huge number of brand new apartments come on the market in the last eighteen months nationwide, and seemingly bundles more to come, judging by the building going on near me. Some have undeniably been a good buy, but by no means all, and there is some evidence to suggest that the market is becoming saturated with this type of property. There's a block of apartments two miles from me that have been available for nearly three years, and they are still advertising: "Last 3 remaining!" They seem to have been saying that since the turn of the century.

I saw a survey just last week that suggested a monster 75% of all people who were living in these kind of flats now hankered after switching into a house with a garden where their kids and pets could run around outside, and where they could sit in the sunshine with a glass of wine and read the Sunday papers. I can believe it too.

Some buy-to-let owners of these flats have been heading for the exits but to their horror, have found they cannot get the money back they paid for them. The future for fancy buy-to-let apartments in some areas looks difficult at best. The message must be: **Be careful!**

I first wrote the previous few paragraphs four years ago, and my, how they resonate today. Flat building has become an epidemic throughout the country in the rush to meet government house building targets and many so called property clubs duly talked unwary investors into buying into the dream by offering unlikely discounts that were purportedly going to cover the deposits. I went to see the guys at HSBC and asked if they would finance apartment buy-to-let mortgages using these so-called discounts as the deposit. They laughed me out of court and invited me to leave. No doubt they are pleased today they did not get over involved in such things, unlike so many other banks that are now desperately foisting rights issues on their shareholders in a desperate attempt to shore up their creaking balance sheets.

Many of these so called property clubs have not surprisingly gone down the tubes, Inside Track, to name but one, Challenor for another, and I am sure there will be many more. I have to admit that at the height of the property boom a year or two ago, even I was beginning to look at some of those flash new apartments being offered with attractive looking discounts that were seemingly available everywhere, but boy, how thankful I am that I never went near them.

As I write, these apartments are plunging in price, and many simply cannot find a buyer. There is a new block that has gone up near me where three months ago large billboard ads proclaimed: **Only 2 remaining**. Yet even to this day only one flat has been taken, so who has been telling porky pies? Surely not the developer? It is hard to have any sympathy for them for they certainly raised their prices at every opportunity and often out of all proportion to the building costs. What goes around comes around! 350,000 unsold flats in the country today, so says my daily newspaper. Rent them out, I say!

But this is not all bad news for the new buy-to-let investor. Why? Because there will come a point when these properties are discounted too much by desperate people who just want rid. One day they will become a good buy. May be we haven't reached that stage yet. Last week (July 2008) I was offered a modernised one bedroom ground floor apartment in a big English city for a discounted price of... 54,000!

When was the last time we saw new properties coming on the open market at that kind of price? A good while ago that's for sure, yet many shrewd operators don't think we have hit the bottom yet. This morning I was offered a modernised three bedroom house for 59,950! Keep a look out. Bargains will be found.

One great point from dropping prices is that the deposit required, even if it is 15% or 20%, is a lot less to find than it once was, meaning that buy-to-let properties are once again becoming within the range of more potential investors who were priced out when values were sky rocketing.

One thing is for sure, before prices begin to rise again, whenever that will be, there will be some juicy bargains to be had. Keep a close eye on things in your area. Try and read the market. Are prices dropping or rising? This is vital market intelligence that will help you to make your financial decisions when the time comes.

In some areas these modern apartments are already turning up as distressed sales in property auctions and I suspect we are just beginning to see the tip of the iceberg. But who's complaining if great deals are to be found at auction. You might like to check out these property auction houses, but don't be railroaded into paying very high prices for paper catalogues that can often be downloaded for free across the Internet. And never be rushed into buying property at auction where the quick-fire electric atmosphere has caught out many a beginner over the years.

Allsop & Co. www.allsop.co.uk
Andrews & Robertson. www.a-r.co.uk
Athawes, Son & Co. www.athawesauctioneers.co.uk
Barnard Marcus. www.barnardmarcus.co.uk
Countrywide. www.countrywidepropertyauctions.co.uk
Drivers & Norris. www.drivers.co.uk
Clive Emson. www.cliveemson.co.uk
FPD Savills. www.fpdsavills.co.uk
Halifax Property Auctions. www.halifax.co.uk
Harman Healy. www.harman-healy.co.uk
Keith Pattinson Ltd. www.pattinson.co.uk
Nelson Bakewell. www.nelson-bakewell.co.uk
Roy Pugh & Co. www.pugh-company.co.uk
Strettons. www.strettons.co.uk
Venmore Thomas & Jones. www.vtj.co.uk
Ward & Partners. www.wardandpartners.co.uk

Many of the purpose built apartments that have struggled to sell are now flooding on to the lettings market, and they are great properties for any agent to acquire because they are virtually maintenance free, attract a high quality tenant, a good rental, and there are plenty to go round. Don't miss out on your share!

CHEAP PROPERTY CAN ALWAYS GO CHEAPER

I know of a chap who bought a former council house in Hull a few years for 22,500. He couldn't believe that properties could sell for such a price. On the face of it, it looked a good deal, a reasonably well-built three-bedroom semi detached house with gardens and central heating.

A few years later he had it valued by an independent estate agent. They now said it was worth 14,500, if he could find a buyer. Remember, no matter how low prices appear, in certain circumstances, they can always go lower.

There have been numerous complaints aired in the newspapers about some of these companies and property clubs, often ironically in the same papers that continue to run the advertisements. The complaints usually centre on poor property management and poor rental returns. One such beef in Ian Hetherington's column in the Mail on Sunday was from a person who bought a house on the promise that rental payments from Housing Benefit would be forthcoming at 325.00 per month.

In fact payments took an age to start, and when they did come through they were only for 250.00 per month, not even covering the mortgage payment. Clearly the agent concerned was not following our advice to collect the shortfall from the tenant. Several of these companies have since closed down and disappeared. Much money has been lost. Much money has vanished. These companies are not regulated; though methinks it won't be so long before they are. Be warned, do your homework thoroughly. Caveat Emptor – Buyer Beware.

Some of the dirt cheap properties being touted were often located in what used to be described as depressed areas. Hull, Gateshead, Sunderland, Burnley and Blackburn have all been rich sources for the supply of cheap housing in recent times. But the north of England in general in the last few years has NOT been a housing black spot when it came to house values.

Don't believe me? Well look at this. I bought a three bedroom terraced house in central Birkenhead, an archetypal northern industrial town, for 16,500 in the year 2000. You won't be surprised to learn that it needed refurbishing. When I'd finished it, it stood me 25,000 all in and it was valued at 36,500. Not a bad return you might think, until you see that in June 2005 the house next door, an almost identical property, went on the market for 90,500! And this is in Birkenhead, and anyone who has been there will know that this is not exactly Beverley Hills! Northern industrial towns did not as a whole experience poor house prices, so you have to ask yourself again, why are the houses being touted by some of the property clubs so cheap?

The answer is clear, because no one wants to live in them. The chances are they are located in half empty streets with the windows boarded up. Former council estates now almost completely abandoned to the joy riders and drug dealers who inhabit the streets after dark. If you don't believe me, get in your car, or jump on the train and go and see for yourself.

CHECK LOCATIONS WITH YOUR OWN EYES

At least that way you will reassure yourself that the properties you are becoming involved with are viable propositions. While you are in the area, stay somewhere overnight, and drive, or stroll, if you are brave enough, down the streets at ten o' clock at night and really get a feel for the place. If you feel uncomfortable, ill at ease, unsafe even, or intimidated in those areas, then how do you think the potential tenant would feel? Your tenant, remember. Precisely the same I would think.

Northern towns are exactly the same as anywhere else in that there are many roads that anyone would be happy to live in, and some roads where you definitely would not. If you are buying from your chair a hundred or two hundred miles away, how do you know what sort of streets they are in? You don't! The reason these properties are so cheap, for the most part, is because they are in the roads that nobody else, particularly the locals, want to live in. And if the locals don't want to live there, who in heck is going to rent them?

These run down difficult areas don't even have to be located in northern English towns either. A few years ago I received details of cheap properties available in Holywell in North Wales. I jumped in the car and drove there and took a look at them.

I was amazed. The houses were substantial enough semi detached properties, clearly formerly council owned, but in one street alone I counted eight out of the ten houses were boarded up and abandoned. Graffiti covered the boarded windows. A smouldering burnt out car sat half on the pavement and half on the road. A group of obviously bored and unemployed surly youths were lighting cigarettes and were watching my every move. The former tenants had probably bought them under the council right to buy scheme and at the first available opportunity had fled the neighbourhood to live somewhere nicer. There would have to be an enormous number of improvements to persuade anyone to live in those houses now. I reckon they could easily be bulldozed. They might be dirt-cheap, but would you buy them? Would you live there? I doubt it. I wouldn't.

Five minutes drive away were large beautiful detached houses selling for 200,000 plus, with fantastic views out over the Dee estuary towards the Wirral peninsula. There are streets you'd buy in, and there are streets where you wouldn't. Check out the locations you are buying in yourself, in person, before you commit to anything. To do otherwise would be foolish in the extreme. Never trust other people to do it for you, and never buy anything unless you have seen it for yourself.

DEAL DIRECT WITH REPUTABLE ESTATE AGENTS

If you still believe buying in these areas is a good idea, get hold of the local newspapers and deal directly with a reputable local estate agent. You don't need impressively named property companies and clubs to do it for you. They will only charge you a fat fee for the privilege.

Established estate agents will always give you plenty of free advice as to whether a property will rent or not, and these people are heavily regulated. Is Dick's Property Club subject to the same strict regulation? No. It isn't. Whatever you do, don't part with any cash to a third party on the back of great promises. You might never see it again. Some of these clubs and associations charged huge fees, often far more than a long established estate agent would ever think of doing, and you have to ask yourself precisely what you are getting for this money. Usually they justify their fees by creating a nominal discount on the asking price. But are these discounts real or imaginary? A good question. I know what I think. What do you think?

My advice would be to concentrate on buying in the areas you know. After all, you have now become a property expert yourself, the biggest property expert in YOUR town, so why would you even consider becoming involved with a company of whom you know little, in a town where you know even less, to purchase a property in a road that could be totally unsellable and unletable? It doesn't make a lot of sense does it?

COUNCIL PROPERTY CAN BE GOOD VALUE

Not all council properties are bad buys, far from it. There are former local authority houses on council estates I wouldn't hesitate to snap up, because I know the estates where people want to live. That's the kind of market intelligence you will garner in your area as you become more aware of what is going on around you.

Don't assume that everyone has this knowledge, they don't. You can make the most of your expertise in your own backyard by backing your judgement, and I am confident when the time comes, you will buy the right property. When buying to let, buy the exactly same type of properties where you were inundated with applications from tenants wishing to rent. That way, you know for sure that your house will always be full and the rent and the mortgage payments will be paid.

Before you part with any cash don't forget to have a survey carried out to highlight any deficiencies. That money is always well spent. And when you look at the survey, look at it with open eyes. Don't immediately assume the house is a non-runner if there are jobs that need putting right. The surveyor is paid good money to find fault with properties, and it would be a very rare house indeed if the report came back with EVERTHING IS FINE! It is quite normal for the surveyor to find some faults; it is up to you as the potential buyer to evaluate how serious they are. Do your arithmetic again, try to get a discount on the asking price to cover the cost of putting things right, don't run away from a deal until you are sure the figures don't add up.

To recap:

Operate in the areas you know
Check out every property in person
Never part with money
to people you don't know
Always have a survey done
If it looks too good to be true, it probably is!

Twenty-Five:
Houses of Multiple Occupation – HMO's

Personally, I would not touch Houses of Multiple Occupation, (HMO's) under any circumstances. Why? Because they are a whole new ball game, legally speaking, and in England at least, you will need to apply for, and gain an appropriate licence before you can manage such a property. Things can get complicated before and after that.

Yet I can see certain circumstances where you might wish to become involved, where you might become tempted. Firstly, you might have inherited such a beast from a family forebear. In that case, you can't just abandon it. Secondly, one of your favourite landlords might have several such HMO's already up and running, and they might ask you to manage them. It can be very difficult to say no.

Thirdly, one single property might have as many as thirty separate rooms and tenants, and you can already see those dosh signs twinkling in your mind. You would, quite rightly, be reluctant to turn them down, because if you did, they might well end up with Bentall's Rentals on the other side of town, and you would do anything to stop Bentall's Rentals getting their sticky feelers anywhere near your territory.

So here are some brief guidelines on HMO's. And first up, what exactly is an HMO?

Under the Housing Act of 2004 if you let a property which is one of the following, it **is** an HMO. It isn't for you to decide.

- An entire house or flat that is let to three or more tenants who form two or more households and who share a kitchen, bathroom or toilet

- A house that has been converted entirely into bedsits or other non-self-contained accommodation and which is let to three or more tenants who form two or more households and share kitchen, bathroom, or toilet

- A converted house which contains one or more flats which are not wholly self-contained. (i.e. the flat does not contain a kitchen, bathroom or toilet)

- A building that is converted entirely into self contained flats if the conversion did not meet the standards of the 1991 Building Regulations, and more than one third of the flats are let on short-term tenancies

I did warn you it could get complicated! Mandatory licensing has been introduced to raise standards of accommodation in the rented sector and in order to obtain a licence, the local housing authority must be satisfied that:

- The proposed licence holder (you!) is a fit and proper person
- Is the most appropriate person to hold the licence
- That proper management standards are applied to the property

- That the HMO is suitable, or can be made suitable, for occupation by the number of tenants allowed under the licence with at least the minimum prescribed standards of amenities and facilities

The licensing application form contains questions which enable the local hosing authority to decide whether or not the landlord or agent, meet the criteria and can be duly awarded a licence.

Still want more information? I thought you might! Go here and check out everything they have to say: http://www.communities.gov.uk/publications/housing/li censinghousestenants

Last time I looked there were some free leaflets and booklets available. In practice, HMO's are usually let to students, casual workers, recently arrived immigrants, many of whom can't speak English that well, if at all, and the like. Collecting rental on HMO's can sometimes be a stressful exercise in itself. Maintenance matters too can often take longer than on single let properties, and you can certainly expect to spend far more time on these kinds of projects than on straight Assured Shorthold ones.

If you do take on any HMO's you should ensure that you are adequately rewarded for the considerable extra time and stress that you will undoubtedly expend on such management.

One thing is clear: you cannot and must not, let out HMO's without obtaining the necessary licence and expertise. To obtain that, you will need to do some considerable additional homework. Don't let over zealous landlords bully you into taking them on. Sometimes landlords are only too pleased to get rid of the management of HMO's because these type of properties can be so troublesome and time consuming.

Over the years I have received many frantic emails from landlords and agents who have got themselves into a jam or fix of some kind, asking for my advice. I am happy to provide it, subject to time constraints, but I note that most of them have one thing in common, they were mainly to do with problems with HMO's, and that says it all.

As I said at the start, I would not be interested in these kind of properties myself, but ultimately, it is your business, and someone has to manage them, and some people make good money with them, but this is another decision that only you can decide. If you venture down this road, I wish you all the luck with it, but as in so many things, it hinges on doing more than adequate research beforehand.

Twenty-Six:
Your 21 Income Stream Business

As your business grows and prospers you could develop it into a 21-income stream business. True, you may decide to pass on certain aspects, but they are all there for you if you decide to incorporate them. To recap, they include:

- Tenants processing fees
- Landlords, who don't want management, one off fee
- Landlords, under management initial fee
- Landlords, monthly management fee
- Insurance premiums commission
- Commission on buy-to-let mortgages
- Renewing tenancy agreements
- Preparing Inventories
- Providing Housing Benefit consultations
- Property Maintenance work for your landlords and others
- Solving landlords and tenants disputes
- Selling space on your property website to private individuals
- Selling space on your property website to other agents
- Earning commission through click through banners
- Reducing costs on utility bills
- Interest on positive cash flow
- Revenue on HMO's managed
- Preparing tenancy agreements for third parties
- Commission on properties that you have sold for others
- Collecting rental on the properties you now own
- Making money on properties you have bought to refurbish and sell on

It's an impressive list, and in any twelve-month period I would expect to earn money in all twenty-one sections, with the possible exception of HMO's.

The secret to running a profitable business, in property or anything else, is to screw down the overheads as low as possible, keep the margins as high as you can, and introduce new revenue streams whenever you see them, especially ones that cost little to start, and take up minimal time.

Combine that with low risk and practically no bad debt and you have a winning formula. Property letting and management **is** a winning formula and it is no surprise to me that the national groups such as Belvoir, Martin & Co, and Link-Up amongst others have enjoyed great success. They still have aggressive expansion plans across the nation and even overseas. They are looking to grow bigger still and become even more prosperous, and so could you - without the need for many thousands of pounds of royalty payments and sign-up fees.

To recap:

Seek Out New Revenue Streams
Especially ones that require Little Work
Keep an Open Mind
Keep up with Changing Trends
Monitor Your Competitors
What are they doing that is New?

Twenty-Seven:
Stamp Duty

If you bought or saw the original edition of SPLAM! you may remember there was a whole chapter on the ins and outs of Stamp Duty with regard to letting residential property in Britain.

The good news is that Stamp Duty on assured shorthold lets in Britain has now been abolished, providing the total rental does not exceed 60,000 per annum on that particular property.

It is one headache and expense that you and your landlords can consign to the dustbin of history, at least for now, but who is to say that at some point it might not return. Let's hope not. If only we could get Stamp Duty abolished or significantly reduced on buying! Fat chance! But we can dream, can't we?

For now, on lettings, you can forget it. Move on.

Twenty-Eight:
So That's All
There Is To It?

You now know everything there is to know about buying, selling, and renting property in Britain today. But of course, you don't! Qualified surveyors spend five years, and more, training and still don't know everything, so reading one book will only scratch the surface.

I liken the property industry to the planet Jupiter. Huge and cloudy, swirling, forever changing; always on the move, magnificent and mysterious. You will NEVER know all there is to know about property, no one ever does, no one ever will, circumstances change, legislation changes. It's up to you to educate yourself and keep abreast of the latest developments.

Joining a trade association is an ideal way to do this as they will send you huge quantities of paperwork, magazines, memos, bulletins, probably more than you can cope with, and they will give you access to their members' only sections on their websites. They are not cheap to join, but are invaluable, and I strongly recommend you join at least one association. You could do worse than join the Landlord Zone here: www.landlordzone.co.uk and sign up for their free newsletters.

Read everything you can lay your hands on, and study. Learn from your own deals and lettings; learn from your mistakes, for you will surely make some along the way. The best education of all is practical. You will certainly learn far more from your actual transactions, both the successful ones, and the less so, than I or anyone else could ever show you.

But you do now have sufficient knowledge to set about launching you own property letting and management business. And you could do that with only a few hundred seed capital. You now have many contacts and sources of information where you could increase your expertise. You have the sources required to obtain tenancy agreements and all the necessary related documentation.

You know where and how to locate properties, you know how to set about your advertising, you know what to say to landlords and tenants alike, and you know what your primary target is: To become the <u>BEST</u> letting agent in the town or county, **no less**, and that won't be as hard to accomplish as you might think. Some of your competitors will be hot, really hot, and difficult to topple, but equally, some of them will be old, tired and disinterested. That's very good news for you. You certainly now know far more than I did when I first started, and if I could go on to successfully rent, refurbish and sell thousands of properties, then why couldn't you? There is absolutely no reason at all. I don't have a property qualification. It didn't stop me.

Enjoy your business, keep a smile on your face, remain optimistic and determined, provide an efficient, honest and ethical service, forever seek to improve in all things, both personally, and your business skills, and you **will** be successful. If you are anything like me, you will rush through this book, then toss it to one side, intent on getting started straight away, and there is nothing wrong with a sense of urgency, but do make a note to return to these pages every week, every month or so, at least in the early days, and check your progress with that outlined here. In the heat of the battle it's so easy to forget a particular aspect of any business, and regular revision always pays dividends.

I would welcome your feedback on any aspect covered in this publication. Your comments may be incorporated in future editions of this work. I'd especially like to hear from you if there is any particular area you would like me to cover in more detail, or indeed if there's any facet I haven't touched upon.

Keep an eye on our website www.splam.co.uk where we will post articles, information and updates on property matters and where through the site you can contact me if you have anything you want to contribute. At the time of writing all the Internet links within this publication are checked and live, so if you bought the download version, you can simply click through. If they don't work, they have changed.

Thanks so much for staying through to the end, and good luck with all your property dealings in the future. I wish you well, and of course, great success too. You will achieve it, I am confident of that.

Trade Directory

AFFILIATE MARKETING COMPANIES

www.affiliatemarketing.co.uk
www.affiliatefuel.com
www.cj.com
www.paidonresults.com
www.ukaffiliates.com
www.tradedoubler.com

AUCTIONEERS

Allsop & Co. www.allsop.co.uk
Andrews & Roberston. www.a-r.co.uk
Athawes, Son & Co. www.athawesauctioneers.co.uk
Barnard Marcus. www.barnardmarcus.co.uk
Countrywide. www.countrywidepropertyauctions.co.uk
Drivers & Norris. www.drivers.co.uk
Clive Emson. www.cliveemson.co.uk
FPD Savills. www.fpdsavills.co.uk
Halifax Property Auctions. www.halifax.co.uk
Harman Healy. www.harman-healy.co.uk
Keith Pattinson Ltd. www.pattinson.co.uk
Nelson Bakewell. www.nelson-bakewell.co.uk
Roy Pugh & Co. www.pugh-company.co.uk
Strettons. www.strettons.co.uk
Venmore Thomas & Jones. www.vtj.co.uk
Ward & Partners. www.wardandpartners.co.uk

COMPUTER SOFTWARE SUPPLIERS – PROPERTY SPECIALISTS

CARL
Computer Aided Residential Lettings
84 Beal Lane
Shaw, Lancs OL2 8BH
Tel: 0845 345 5591
Fax: 01706 880800
www.carlcomms.co.uk
Email: info@carlcomms.co.uk

EZPZ Software Ltd.
www.ezpzsoftware.co.uk

Property Management Software
www.fondue.co.uk
www.landlordzone.co.uk
www.propertyhawk.co.uk
www.propertyintellect.com
www.propertymanageronline.com
www.propertyportfoliosoftware.co.uk
Rentman: www.rman.co.uk

CREDIT CHECKING AND REFERENCING AGENCIES

Homelet
Tel: 0845 117 6000
Fax: 0845 117 6001
www.homelet.co.uk

Letsure
www.letsure.co.uk

DEPOSIT PROTECTION INFORMATION

www.direct.gov.uk/en/TenancyDeposit

HOUSES OF MULTIPLE OCCUPATION - HMO's

www.communities.gov.uk/housing/rentingandletting

HOUSING BENEFIT INFORMATION

www.dwp.gov.uk/lifeevent/benefits/housing_benefit.asp

PROFESSIONAL INDEMNITY INSURANCE

Hanover Park Commercial Limited
Phoenix House
Wellesley Road
Croydon CR0 2NW
Tel: 0845 345 0815
Web: www.hanover-park.co.uk

Professional Indemnity insurance may also be
Available through the various trade and landlord
associations

PROPERTY INSURANCE POLICIES

Homelet
Tel: 0845 117 6000
Fax:0845 117 6001
www.homelet.co.uk

Letsure
www.letsure.co.uk

The National Federation of Landlords
www.nfrl.org.uk

REDUCED PRICED UTILITIES

Telecom Plus PLC
www.telecomplus.org.uk

SALES & RENTAL WEBSITES

www.assertahome.com
www.cdproperty.co.uk
www.dauntons.co.uk
www.davisestates.co.uk
www.excel-property.co.uk
www.fish4homes.co.uk
www.foxtons.co.uk
www.halfapercent.com
www.home.co.uk
www.home-sale.co.uk
www.hotproperty.co.uk
www.lettingsearch.co.uk
www.lettingweb.co.uk
www.lookproperty.co.uk
www.net-lettings.co.uk
www.paramountproperties.co.uk
www.pebblebeachmedia.co.uk
www.primelocation.com
www.propertyadsonline.co.uk
www.propertyfinder.com
www.propertylive.co.uk
www.propertymatters.co.uk
www.rentalsandsales.co.uk
www.rightmove.co.uk

www.simplyrent.co.uk
www.themovechannel.com
www.torent.co.uk
www.ukpropertyguide.co.uk
www.ukpropertyshop.co.uk
www.worldwidecottages.com

AMERICAN:

www.californiarealestate.com
www.estateround.com
www.foxtons.com
www.floridarealestate.com
www.homes.com
www.homeseekers.cyberhomes.com
www.househunt.com
www.newyorkrealestate.com
www.realtor.com
www.remax.com
www.us-realestatedirectory.com

WORLDWIDE:

www.aquavista.com
www.greenlightproperties.co.uk
www.planetrealestate.com
www.propertyforsaleguide.com
www.propertyworld.com
www.worldwidepropertyshop.net
www.worldwidecottages.com
www.worldwiderealestate.com

STAMP DUTY OFFICES

Belfast Stamp Office
Ground Floor
Dorchester House
52 – 58 Great Victoria Street
Belfast BT2 7QE
Tel: 028 90 505127

Birmingham Stamp Office
5th Floor, Norfolk House
Smallbrook Queensway
Birmingham B5 4LA
Tel: 0121 633 3313

Bristol Stamp Office
The Pithay
All Saints Street
Bristol BS1 2NY
Tel: 0117 927 2022

Edinburgh Stamp Office
Grayfield House, Spur X
5 Bankhead Avenue
Edinburgh EH11 4AE
Tel: 0131 442 3161

London Stamp Office:
Personal Callers Only to:
South West Wing
Bush House
Strand
London WC2B 4QN
Tel: 0207 438 7252 or 7452

Manchester Stamp Office
Upper 5th floor
Royal Exchange
Exchange Street
Manchester M2 7EB
Tel: 0161 834 8020

Newcastle Stamp Office
4th Floor
Weardale House
Washington
Tyne and Wear NE37 1LW
Tel: 0191 261 1199

Worthing Stamp Office
Postal Applications Only
Room 35, East Block
Barrington Road
Worthing, Sussex
Tel: 01903 508962

Website address for all stamp duty queries:
www.inlandrevenue.gov.uk/so

SIGN MANUFACTURERS

www.agencyexpress.co.uk
www.estate-signs.co.uk
www.curtisscreenprint.co.uk

STATIONERY SUPPLIERS

Neat Ideas

www.neat-ideas.com
Tel: 01302 890089

Staples Stationery
www.staples.co.uk
FREE Tel hotline: 0800 6929292

Viking Direct
Freephone: 0800 424444
Fax: 0800 622211
www.viking-direct.co.uk

TRADE ORGANISATIONS & ASSOCIATIONS

ARLA
The Association of Residential Letting Agents
www.arla.co.uk

The Landlord Zone
www.landlordzone.co.uk

The Law Society
www.lawsociety.org.uk

NAEA
The National Association of Estate Agents
www.naea.co.uk

The National Association of Realtors (USA)
www.realtor.org

The National Landlords Association
www.landlords.org.uk

NFRL
The National Federation of Residential Landlords
www.nfrl.org.uk

The Royal Institute of Chartered Surveyors
www.rics.org.uk

TRAINING FOR PROFESSIONALS
Tel: 01258 858585
Email: tfplettingnetwork.com

UKALA
The United Kingdom Association of Letting Agents
www.ukala.org.uk

TRADE PUBLICATIONS

The Estates Gazette
Britain's oldest property magazine founded in 1858
www.estatesgazettegroup.com

The Agreement Magazine
Obtain through the Association of Residential Letting
Agents at
www.arla.co.uk

The Estate Agent Magazine
Order through the National Association of Estate Agents
at
www.naea.co.uk

Lettings Update
Available through the UK Association of Letting Agents
www.ukala.org.uk

WEB DESIGN SERVICES

www.partnershop.co.uk/shop/1598

Web names registered from just £1.99. Hosting from just £4 per month. Design templates and comprehensive help files. Design your own sites for very little outlay.

WEB TRAFFIC GENERATOR PROGRAMS

www.trafficswarm.com/go.cgi?279577
www.freenetleads.com/free/1138car

- Please note that any contact listed here is not necessarily a recommendation. Some of these companies I have never personally used.

At-A-Glance Conversion Table Weekly Rental To Monthly

Weekly	Monthly:
£50 weekly rental equates to	£216.66
£55	£238.33
£60	£260.00
£65	£281.66
£70	£303.33
£75	£325.00
£80	£346.66
£85	£368.33
£90	£390.00
£95	£411.66
£100	£433.33
£105	£455.00
£110	£476.66
£115	£498.33
£120	£520.00
£125	£541.66
£130	£563.33
£135	£585.00
£140	£606.66
£145	£628.33
£150	£650.00

£155	£671.66
£160	£693.33
£165	£715.00
£170	£736.66
£175	£758.33
£180	£780.00
£185	£801.66
£190	£823.33
£195	£845.00
£200	£866.66
£205	£888.33
£210	£910.00
£215	£931.66
£220	£953.33
£225	£975.00
£230	£996.66
£235	£1018.33

Glossary of Trade Terms and Abbreviations

ARLA: Association of Residential Letting Agents
AST: Assured Shorthold Tenancy
CH: Centrally heated
COMPLETION: The day when transfer of ownership of a property takes place (on purchases and sales)
CONVEYANCING: Legal term for the buying and selling process
COVENANTS: rules and regulations governing the property contained in its title deeds or its lease
CORGI: The Confederation for the Registration of Gas Installers
DG: Double glazed
DILAPIDATION: A claim made against the tenant for damage and excessive wear to a property
DIP: Decision in principle
DISBURSEMENTS: the fees that your solicitor has to pay such as stamp duty, land registration and search fees (on purchases and sales)
DPC: Damp proof course
DSS: Department of Social Security. The body responsible for the paying of Housing Benefit
E & O E: Errors and omissions excepted
EXCHANGE OF CONTRACTS: This is the point at which both the buyer and seller are legally bound by the deal (on purchases and sales)
FF: fully furnished
F&F: Fixtures and fittings
FFF: First floor flat
GAZUMPING: Where a vendor accepts a higher offer from a third party even if they have accepted an offer

already. This is legal if they have not already exchanged contracts

GCH: Gas central heating

GF: Ground floor

GROUND RENT: The annual charge payable by the leaseholders to the owner of the freehold

FREEHOLD: land and/or buildings held by owner in absolute possession

FRI: Full repairing and insuring lease

HBO: Housing benefit office

IPT: Insurance premium tax

LAND REGISTRATION FEE: Fee paid to verify legal title and rights over a property and to register the ownership of a property with the Land Registry

LEASE: A contract by which land or buildings is conveyed for a specific time by its owner (the lessor) to tenant (the lessee) normally for rent

LEASEHOLDER: A person having tenure over a property by lease

LTV: Loan to value. The loan is expressed as a % of the purchase price or valuation

MP: Monthly premium

NAEA: National Association of Estate Agents

NEGATIVE EQUITY: Is where the mortgage on the property exceeds the value of the property

NICEIC: National Inspection Council of Electrical Installation Contracting

OA: Offers above

OIEO: Offers in excess of

OIRO: Offers in the region of

O/O: Offers over

OPP: Outline planning permission

PCM: Per calendar month

PF: Partly furnished

POA: Price on application

PI: Professional Indemnity (Insurance)

PP: Planning permission

PTD: Pre tenancy determination, procedure whereby the benefit office will advise what portion of the rental they will pay, prior to the tenant taking up occupation

REPOSSESSION: Happens when the borrower defaults on the mortgage and the lender legally enforces a sale to recover their debt

RICS: Royal Institute of Chartered Surveyors

SCHEDULE: Notification of housing benefit payments, usually 4-weekly

SDLT: Stamp Duty Land Tax, the replacement for traditional Stamp Duty on assured shorthold tenancies.

SOM: Standing Order Mandate

SPLAM: Successful Property Letting And Management

STAMP DUTY: Duty imposed by the government on certain types of legal documents and transactions, such as property deals

STRUCTURAL SURVEY: A full report on the condition of the property, carried out by a qualified surveyor

TENANCY: Period of holding land or property as a tenant

TITLE DEEDS: The documents that show who has the title or right of ownership to a property

UKALA: United Kingdom Association of Letting Agents

UNDER OFFER: A property that has an offer accepted by the vendor, but the two parties have not yet exchanged contracts

UNF: Unfurnished

UNSECURED LOAN: A loan where no security has been offered by the buyer to the lender.

If you have any comments regarding this book, feedback of any kind, ideas and suggestions for any sequels that may be published, we would like to hear from you. You can contact us at
supalife@aol.com

For updates and property articles please check out our website
www.splam.co.uk